S0-AVI-241

nihongo notes 2

expressing oneself in japanese

by
osamu mizutani
nobuko mizutani

The Japan Times

ISBN4-7890-0098-2

Copyright © 1979 by Osamu Mizutani and Nobuko Mizutani

All rights reserved, including the right to reproduce this book
or portions thereof in any form.

First edition: April 1979
18th printing: May 2001

Jacket design by Koji Detake

Published by The Japan Times, Ltd.
5-4, Shibaura 4-chome, Minato-ku, Tokyo 108-0023, Japan
Phone: 03-3453-2013
http://www.bookclub.japantimes.co.jp/

Printed in Japan

FOREWORD

This book is a compilation of the seventy columns which appeared in *The Japan Times* from December 3rd, 1977 to April 1st, 1979 under the title "Nihongo Notes." (The preceding set of seventy columns was published in 1977 as *Nihongo Notes 1*.) A section of polite conversational expressions has been added to supplement the columns.

The columns in this volume, like the ones in *Nihongo Notes 1*, are designed to explain how the Japanese use their language to communicate with each other. While continuing to deal with the actual usage of various Japanese expressions, we attempt in this volume to provide more detailed explanations. In other words, we are concerned with specific situations such as how the Japanese start business discussion, how they develop and conclude discussions, and how they make requests and criticize others.

It is a great pleasure for us to have readers who share our interest in communication; we hope this volume will be of some help to those attempting to fully understand and express themselves well in Japanese.

We would like to acknowledge the help of Janet Ashby who checked the English for these columns and offered us valuable suggestions just as she did for the first volume.

April, 1979
Osamu and Nobuko Mizutani

CONTENTS

4

5

Note Concerning Romanization

The romanization used in this book (as well as in *An Introduction to Modern Japanese*) is based on the Hepburn system with the following modifications.

1. When the same vowel occurs consecutively, the letter is repeated rather than using the "‾" mark.
   ex. *Tookyoo* (instead of *Tōkyō*)
2. The sound indicated by the hiragana ん is written with "*n*" regardless of what sound follows it.
   ex. *shinbun* (instead of shimbun)
   ex. *shinpai* (instead of shimpai)

The words connected with hyphens are pronounced as one unit.
   ex. *genki-desu*
   ex. *Soo-desu-ne*

Sukoshi tsumete-kudasaimasen-ka

すこし　つめてくださいませんか

(Would you please move over a little?)

Yesterday evening Mr. Ernest Lerner was reading a magazine on the train home. There was some space between Mr. Lerner and the man who sat next to him. Then a woman entered, stood in front of this space, and said

Sumimasen-ga.

Mr. Lerner sensed that she wanted to sit down and was quite willing to move over and make room for her. However he was curious to know what expression is used for "Please move over a little," so he waited for her to continue. But the woman said nothing and moved her arm as if sweeping something away. Then the man sitting next to Mr. Lerner quickly moved over to make room for her.

Later Mr. Takada said that a common expression in such cases is

Sukoshi tsumete-kudasaimasen-ka.
すこし　つめてくださいませんか。

(*lit.* Would you please pack yourselves closer together?)

but that it is very common not to use it but merely indicate it nonverbally. Thus this woman didn't use a gesture just because Mr. Lerner was a foreigner.

*   *   *

At first Mr. Lerner thought it was rather rude for the woman to have just moved her hand about, saying nothing. But when he thought it over, he realized that many Japanese often do

8

the same sort of thing. For instance, when he meets people working in the building where his office is located, some of them just bow to him to mean "Hello" instead of saying something. Also, when a man walks in front of others who are sitting, he often holds his arm straight out with the hand held thumb upwards, instead of saying

Shitsuree-shimasu.
(Excuse me.)

When offering tea also, Japanese often just say *Doozo* and use gestures to mean "have some tea." In this way most requests can be made without using any verbal expressions other than *Sumimasen-ga* or *Doozo*.

Mr. Lerner had thought that Japanese do not use gestures as often as Westerners, but he realized that actually Japanese do use gestures quite a lot. The difference is that while Westerners usually use gestures to reinforce verbal expressions, Japanese very often use them to replace verbal expressions.

Yasumu wake-niwa ikanai
やすむ　わけには　いかない
(I can't very well take the day off)

Mr. Takada had caught a bad cold and seemed very tired, so Mr. Lerner suggested that he leave the office early. Mr. Takada thanked him and said

Demo, soo yuu wake-nimo ikimasen-yo.
でも、そう　いう　わけにも　いきませんよ。
(But I can't very well do that.)

When Mr. Lerner asked him why he couldn't, he said that he couldn't very well go home early when the others were working hard. Mr. Lerner thought it was no use for a sick person to stay and just make his sickness worse, but he felt interested in the expression. . . *wake-niwa ikanai.* Sensee had once explained to him that . . . *wake-niwa ikanai* or . . . *wake-nimo ikanai* means that one cannot do something because of social reasons. Now that he had heard Mr. Takada use it Mr. Lerner understood what Sensee had meant.

*　　　*　　　*

Of the several expressions used to state inability, . . . *koto-ga dekinai* and *(yasum)enai* are used in any case when one cannot do something; the reason may be physical, social or emotional, while . . . *wake-niwa ikanai* is used when one cannot do smething because of social reasons. A businessman will say to his wife who asks him to stay home when he has caught a cold,

Yasumu wake-niwa ikanai.
やすむ　わけには　いかない。

10

(I can't very well take the day off.)

because he feels he shouldn't be absent, although his absence may not really inconvenience his colleagues.

When a husband says his wife does not have to buy a new dress, she may say

Demo, konna furui-no kite-iku wake-niwa ikanai-wa.
(I can't very well wear this old thing.)

Although it is physically quite possible to wear it, her feelings make it impossible to do so.

Since . . . *wake-niwa ikanai* is not usually used when something is physically impossible, it will be funny to a Japanese to hear something like

Mada akanboo-da-kara aruku wake-niwa ikanai.

to mean "Since she is still a little baby, she cannot walk." In this case,

. . . *arukenai.*

is appropriate.

Komatta-na

こまつたな

(Oh, I'm troubled)

A few weeks ago a young man came to the office to see Miss Yoshida on some urgent business. When Mr. Takada said that she was out and would not come back for a couple of hours, he said

Soo-desu-ka. Komatta-na.
そうですか。　こまったな。
(Is that so? What should I do? — *lit.* Is that so? Oh, I'm troubled.)

Mr. Lerner had heard that *na* is added to a sentence only in familiar speech, so he thought that this young man was being rather rude to Mr. Takada. But Mr. Takada did not seem offended and kindly offered to help him contact her as soon as possible.

*　　*　　*

There are several particles that are added to the end of sentences to show the speaker's emotions or attitude. *Ne* is used when the speaker expects the listener to agree; *yo* is used when the speaker wants to emphasize his statement. The particle *na* said in a low tone as in

mu
Sa   i
　　-na.

expresses the speaker's emotion in a monologue-like statement. *Samui-na* means "Oh, it's cold" and *Iya-ni natchau-na* means "How disgusting." *Na* is often used in statements that are directed to the speaker himself rather than to the listener.

When the young man said *Komatta-na*, it was said to himself even though actually it was audible to Mr. Takada and Mr. Lerner.

Mr. Lerner had noticed that Japanese often talk to themselves in the midst of a conversation in a different tone and with non-polite expressions such as *Aa, soo-ka* or *Aa, soo yuu wake-ka*. After learning that *na* is often used in such statements, he has noticed this *na* very often, mostly used by men, but sometimes even by women. Mr. Takada often says

A, moo jikan-da-na.
(Oh, it's time already.)

And Miss Yoshida was once heard saying

Iya-da-na, mata machigaeta.
(I hate it. I made a mistake again.)

while correcting her typing. (Women usually use *wa* instead of *na*.)

Why do Japanese often talk to themselves in the midst of a conversation? Sensee said this serves a good purpose. If such remarks as *Komatta-na* are directly turned to the listener he may feel obliged to do something about it, but when it is addressed to the speaker himself, the listener can choose whether to offer help or not. Therefore complaints are often expressed in this way, although some people prefer direct remarks.

If a husband were to say after tasting his coffee *Nurui-na* (It's not warm enough), it is likely that his wife will offer to warm it on her own accord; saying *Nurui-yo* will sound as if he is pressing her to warm it.

13

Gomennasai
ごめんなさい
(I'm sorry)

At the office where Mr. Lerner works, a reception was held yesterday afternoon in honor of an important visitor. Mr. Lerner was asked to give a short speech in Japanese. Since everybody looked very formal, he became rather nervous and made a mistake in pronouncing the guest's name, so he hurriedly apologized, saying

Gomennasai.
ごめんなさい。
(I'm sorry.)

Many of the people there laughed. This helped the people relax, although Mr. Lerner lost some confidence in his Japanese.

Later Mr. Takada said that they had laughed because *Gomennasai* sounds feminine; Miss Yoshida said that it was because the expression sounds childish.

*   *   *

Mr. Lerner should have said

Shitsuree-shimashita.
失礼しました。
(*lit.*, I was rude.)

instead of *Gomennasai*. *Gomennasai* is one of those expressions that are used mostly at home between family members, while *Shitsuree-shimashita* is used in social situations. Little children usually apologize to their parents or teachers by saying *Gomennasai*, but *Shitsuree-shima-*

14

shita is not usually used between family members. (*Sumimasen* is also used in apology. It is less formal than *Shitsuree-shimashita* and is used both inside and outside of one's home, by adults or older boys and girls; if a little child said *Sumimasen* to his parents it would sound rather strange.)

Outside of the home, *Gomennasai* is used mainly in family-like situations. Most often it is used by children; among adults, it is often used in informal conversation. For instance, a child will say it to a stranger whose foot he has stepped on by mistake in the train. An elderly person may say it to a younger person even when working at the office unless he has to be formal.

The distinction between formal or social expressions such as *Shitsuree-shimashita* and familiar expressions such as *Gomennasai* seems to be becoming looser. Some people have started using familiar expressions, either intentionally or unintentionally, in formal or social situations. But still it is important to choose appropriate expressions according to the situation if you want to be a really good speaker of Japanese.

Sonna koto-o yuu mon-ja arimasen

そんな ことを いう もんじゃ ありません

(You should not say such a thing)

The other day Mr. Lerner was asked to have dinner at the Takadas. When the family members were talking after dinner, the son said something criticizing his father. Then his mother said

Kodomo-wa sonna koto-o yuu mon-ja arimasen.
こどもは そんな ことを いう もんじゃ ありません。
(*lit.* A child is not a thing to say such a thing.)

Mr. Lerner understood that she had admonished her son, but didn't understand why she had used the word *mono* in referring to her child. Why didn't she use *hito* (person) instead of *mono* (thing)?

*   *   *

The word *mono* (often contracted to *mon* in conversation) is used in various ways. One usage is to mean "be supposed to do (or be) something." *Yuu mon-desu* means "You are supposed to say it" and *Yuu mon-ja arimasen* means "You're not supposed to say it." When Mrs. Takada said *Kodomo-wa sonna koto-o yuu mon-ja arimasen*, she meant that to say such a thing is not appropriate for a child.

This expression . . . *mon-desu* or . . . *mono-ja arimasen* is often used by older people to admonish younger people. A mother will often say to her child

Sonna hon-o yomu mon-ja arimasen.

(You should not read such a book.)
or
Okyaku-sama-niwa aisatsu-suru mon-desu.
(You should greet our guests.)

A teacher of a high school may say to his students

Gakusee-wa motto benkyoo-suru mono-da.
(Students should study harder.)

Even after one has grown up and started working, he may be admonished by older people who will say

Konna yarikata-o suru mon-ja nai.
(This isn't the way you should do it.)

Sometimes old parents are admonished by their children:

Toshiyori-wa muri-o suru mon-ja nai.
(Old people shouldn't overdo.)

Since this expression is used according to the speaker's sense of propriety, it is difficult to give rules for its usage in Japan today where people's life-styles and sense of values are changing and becoming more varied.

Ja...
じゃ……
(Then...)

At Mr. Lerner's office, the workers often stay after work and chat for a while. Mr. Lerner thinks it would be a much better idea to leave as soon as work is over, but it seems to be rather common in Japan, so yesterday evening he decided to join them and see for himself.

They talked about various things for half an hour, when Mr. Takada looked up at the clock and said

Ja, boku-wa...
じゃ、ぼくは……
(*lit.* Then, I...)

and stood up. The others said good-bye and continued their talk. After there was a short silence Miss Yoshida said

Ja, watashi-mo...
じゃ、わたしも……
(*lit.* Then, me too...)

and left. Soon after that everybody left the office, including Mr. Lerner.

Mr. Lerner felt interested in this use of *ja*. The dictionary says that it is a contracted form of *dewa*, which means "then." But to him the Japanese seem to use this word very often without any sentence or phrase that logically precedes "then"; they often start their sentences with *ja* as in

Ja, sorosoro hajimemashoo-ka.

(*lit.* Then, shall we slowly start?)

*   *   *

Ja or *Dewa* (or, sometimes *Sore-ja*) means "then" or "in that case." It is used in responses as in

A: *Moo juuji-desu-yo.* (It's already ten o'clock.)
B: *Ja, dekakemashoo.* (Then let's go.)

But very often *ja* appears not as a reply, but to start a sentence. For instance, when leaving one often says *Ja. . .* or **Ja, kore-de** (*lit.* Then, with this). When starting a meeting or discussion one often says *Ja, hajimemashoo* (Then let's start). To foreigners *Ja* seems to be used with no substantial meaning.

But it has the meaning of "then" in the Japanese mind. When Mr. Takada said *Ja*, he had looked at the clock. The clock showed that it was time for him to leave and the others saw that he had looked at it; thus looking at the clock meant "It's time to leave," and so it is followed by "Then, I'm leaving." There had been a short silence among the company when Miss Yoshida used it, and the people took it as something that made Miss Yoshida appropriately say *Ja*. It can be paraphrased as "the discussion seems to have come to an end; then I will leave."

Thus either nonverbal action or silence precedes the use of *Ja*. If you use it without this, it will seem abrupt to Japanese. In this sense *Ja* corresponds more to the English "Well," as in "Well, shall we go now?"

Naruhodo
なるほど
(Indeed)

Yesterday afternoon Mr. Mori, the director of the company where Mr. Lerner works, was explaining his plan. While listening to him, Mr. Lerner took special care to give *aizuchi* as often as he could. In the past few weeks he has become used to giving *aizuchi*, although not without some effort. This time, he wanted to use some expression other than *Hai*, *Ee* or *Soo-desu-ka*, so he said

Naruhodo.
なるほど。

whenever Mr. Mori paused.

But Mr. Mori did not seem to like this. In fact when Mr. Lerner repeated this expression as *Naruhodo, naruhodo*, he stopped talking and asked him to listen quietly.

Mr. Lerner did not understand what was wrong with his use of *Naruhodo*. Don't Japanese use it very often, especially when listening to others explain things? And even when speaking English, many Japanese seem to say "I see" much too often, perhaps because they regard it as the English equivalent of *Naruhodo*.

*　　　*　　　*

The word *naruhodo* means "indeed," "it's true," or "surely," and is used to show that the speaker has understood perfectly what he has heard. In this sense it is an appropriate word to be used as *aizuchi*, but one has to be very careful when using it in polite speech.

Naruhodo belongs to a group of expressions which are used in a monologue-like way in polite speech, such as *Aa, soo-ka*, or *Aa, soo yuu wake-ka*. When the speaker uses these expressions in the midst of polite conversation, he has to show that they are directed to himself rather than to the listener. In other words, he is permitted to use in polite conversation expressions that are originally familiar only when he is talking to himself. To show this, one has to pronounce such expressions with a lower tone and with a falling intonation; otherwise these expressions sound impolite.

Sometimes people use such expressions on purpose to show their enthusiasm for the conversation. Interviewers on radio or TV programs, for example, often say *Naruhodo* to show that they are so absorbed in the conversation that they have forgotten to pay attention to formalities; by doing this, they can encourage those they are interviewing. (Men use *Naruhodo* in this way more often than women; perhaps women are, or have been so far, trained to refrain from talking to themselves in public.)

Before you are used to this kind of speech, it might be safer to use *Soo-desu-ka* or *Wakarima-shita* in polite speech instead of *Naruhodo*, and use such expressions as

　　Naruhodo, naruhodo.
　　なるほど、なるほど。
　or
　　Naruhodo-nee.
　　なるほどねえ。

only in familiar conversations.

Saa. . .
さあ……
(Well. . .)

When Mr. Lerner was having a cup of coffee with Miss Yoshida and others during the break, Mr. Sato came in. Miss Yoshida asked him several questions about some professional baseball players; Mr. Sato answered all her questions with *Saa . . .* Sometimes he just said

Saa. . . さあ……
(Well. . .)

or

Saa, doo-deshoo-ne.
さあ、どうでしようね。
(Well, I wonder.)

And sometimes he expressed his opinion after saying

Saa, yoku wakarimasen-ga . . .
さあ、よく わかりませんが。
(Well, I don't know, but. . .)

Suddenly Mr. Lerner remembered that Mr. Sato was often called *Saa-san*. Afterwards, Mr. Lerner asked Miss Yoshida if the nickname had been given him because he always answered *Saa . . .* Miss Yoshida laughed and laughed and said that she liked his etymology very much but that it was mistaken. The fact was that he was called *Saa-san* because some girls who worked at the bar where he often went called him by that name (using the first syllable of his last name).

Saa . . . is used when one isn't sure of one's answers or when one cannot make up one's mind. In this sense it corresponds to such English expressions as "Well, I don't know" or "Well, let me think."

Saa . . . can also be used to imply negation. *Saa* . . . alone can mean "Well, I don't think so" or "Well, I'm afraid I can't." In fact it is very often used to avoid saying "No"; saying *Saa* . . . is preferred to saying *lie, shirimasen* (No, I don't know), and *Saa, doo-deshoo-ne* is preferred to *lie, dekimasen* (No, I can't).

And also when giving one's own opinion, Japanese often use *Saa* . . . because being hesitant is usually regarded highly as a sign of modesty. You will hear them say surprisingly often

Saa, yoku wakarimasen-ga.

before expressing themselves.

When used in this way, *Saa* . . . is pronounced with a low tone and a dangling intonation. *Saa* can also be used to urge others to start doing something as in

Saa, dekakemashoo.
(Come, let's go.)

In this case it is pronounced differently, with a high tone and a sharply falling intonation.

Onna-rashii
女らしい
(To be womanly)

A few days ago Miss Yoshida was typing hurriedly. After making a number of mistakes she took the paper from the typewriter, rumpled it, and threw it into the wastebasket which was a few yards away. Mr. Kato, who happened to be passing by, told her that it was

>*Onna-rashiku nai.*
>女らしく　ない。
>(not womanly)

Perhaps he thought that a woman should carry the paper to the wastebasket instead of throwing it from where she was, but Mr. Lerner did not think Miss Yoshida had done something to be criticized for.

When Mr. Lerner talked about it with her later, she said she did not mind because she is used to this kind of criticism from her parents who often say

>*Onna-no kuse-ni. . .*
>女の　くせに……
>(in spite of being a woman)

This made him interested in phrases ending with *-rashii*. Miss Yoshida gave him many examples such as *otoko-rashii* (manly), *kodomo-rashii* (like a child), *sensee-rashii* (like a teacher) and *seejika-rashii* (like a politician). When he asked about *gaijin-rashii* (like a foreigner) she thought a while and said that it could be said, too.

＊　　　＊　　　＊

Such phrases ending with -*rashii* are used to indicate the speaker's judgment that someone follows his expectations of how he should act, and thus they usually imply the speaker's approval. To be *onna-rashii* is desirable while to be *onna-rashiku nai* is undesirable. If a woman does something that is *onna-rashiku nai*, others will often criticize her by saying

Onna-no kuse-ni sonna koto-o. . .
(To do such a thing in spite of being a woman. . .)
. . . *kuse-ni* is used to indicate disapproval and criticism for not behaving as the speaker thinks someone in that category should behave. If a young man acts like an old person, for instance, staying inside on fine days or being too conservative, others will say

Wakai-kuse-ni. . .
(Although he's young. . .)

When someone refers to a teacher as

Sensee-no kuse-ni sensee-rashiku nai.
(Although he's a teacher, he doesn't act like one.)

he may mean that the teacher is not well-versed in his subject, or that he is not properly dressed or that he is overly interested in making money. This depends on what the speaker expects a teacher to be like.

People sometimes like exceptions. While some people like to have experienced politicians, others prefer *seejika-rashiku nai seejika* (a politician who is not like a politician).

Datte. . .

だって……

(Because. . .)

Yesterday the train was delayed for some reason and Mr. Lerner arrived at the office about 10 minutes late. He explained why he was late, saying

Datte densha-ga okureta-n-desu.
だって 電車が おくれたんです。

meaning "Because the train was late." Then Mr. Takada asked him where he had picked up the word *datte*. When he said that he didn't remember, Mr. Takada said that it probably came from Miss Yoshida's speech. Miss Yoshida strongly protested this and said that she would never use such a word at the office. Mr. Takada said that the word sounds feminine and Miss Yoshida said that it is childish.

*　　　*　　　*

Among the several expressions used to indicate reason or cause, *datte* is rather limited in its usage. It is usually used in familiar speech between close friends or between family members; it is not an appropriate expression in polite speech or in more formal social situations.

Datte is used to give a reason while protesting what the other person has said. When asked why he was absent from the office, for example, one usually says

Atama-ga itakatta-node
or
Atama-ga itakatta-n-desu

to mean "Because I had a headache." If someone said

Datte atama-ga itakatta-n-desu.

he would imply that he feels he is being criticized and wants to justify himself. *Datte* can be paraphrased as "You blame me but I have a good reason for . . ." In this sense *datte* can often be translated as "but."

Since *datte* introduces a protesting statement, the sentence following it is usually concluded with such expression as . . .*n-desu*, . . . *da-mono*, . . . *desu-mono*, or . . . *ja arimasen-ka*. All these expressions are used to intensify the speaker's statement.

Thus, if a husband criticizes his wife for not keeping the house clean, she is likely to say

Datte isogashii-n-desu-mono.
だって　いそがしいんですもの。
(But I'm so busy!)
　or
Datte anata, chittomo tetsudatte-kurenai-ja arimasen-ka.
(But you don't help me at all!)

The husband may retort by saying

Datte boku-niwa shigoto-ga aru-n-da-mono.
(But I have my own work to do!)

Shikashi . . .

しかし……

(But . . .)

A few days ago Mr. Okada came to the office to see Mr. Lerner. After they had exchanged *Senjitsu-wa doomo* 's (*lit.* I was rude the other day) and Mr. Okada had taken a seat, he said:

Shikashi samuku narimashita-nee.
しかし　さむく　なりましたねえ。
(But it has become cold, hasn't it?)

Mr. Lerner agreed but he didn't quite understand why Mr. Okada had started the sentence with *shikashi.* They had not talked about anything contradictory to the fact that it had become cold.

*   *   *

Shikashi seems to be used in two ways; one is to introduce a contradictory statement as in:

A: *Fukeeki-desu-nee.* (Business is really bad.)
B: *Ee, shikashi otaku-wa ii-deshoo.* (Yes, but your company must be doing all right.)

Another usage is to show that the speaker wants to drop the topic of conversation and start a new one, as Mr. Okada did in the above case. When one uses *shikashi* in this way, there must be a pause, however short it may be. Since this pause can be very short, it sometimes seems to foreigners that *shikashi* is being used all of a sudden.

In familiar conversation *dakedo* is used in place of *shikashi.* Sometimes *sore-ni shite-mo* (*lit.* even though it is so) is added to either *shi-*

28

kashi or *dakedo* when one uses it to introduce a new topic.

Although it may be easier to understand if one thinks of *shikashi* or *dakedo* as being used in two different ways, actually the two usages mentioned above can be regarded as one. In the first usage, *shikashi* is used to indicate the speaker's denial of the preceding statement, while in the second it is used to show his denial of the preceding topic and his turning to a new one. In fact Japanese do not usually see any difference between the two.

In daily conversation you will hear *shikashi* used surprisingly often in the following sort of way:

(A and B meet on the street.)

A: *Ocha-demo nomimasen-ka.* (Why don't we have some tea?)

B: *Ii-desu-ne. Asoko-wa doo-desu-ka.* (Yes, let's. How about that coffee shop?)

A: *Ee, ja asoko-ni shimashoo.* (Okay. Let's go there.)

(The two start walking to the coffee shop.)

A: *Shikashi Tanaka-san-mo eraku narimashita-nee.* (But Mr. Tanaka has been moving up in the world lately, hasn't he?)

B: *Soo-desu-ne.* (Yes, he has.)

Chotto yuubinkyoku-e itte-kimasu
ちょっと　郵便局へ　いってきます
(I'm going to the post office)

Mr. Lerner asked Sensee how he could make his Japanese sound more natural. Sensee suggested that he use two verbs together — for instance, saying *itte-kimasu* (*lit.* I'll go and come back) instead of *ikimasu* or *yonde-mimasu* (*lit.* I'll read and see) instead of *yomimasu*.

So he started to pay more attention to this in the conversations of the people around him. Yesterday afternoon he heard Miss Yoshida say

Chotto yuubinkyoku-e itte-kimasu-kedo. . .
ちょっと　郵便局へ　いってきますけど……
(I'm going to the post office. — *lit.* I'll go to the post office for a short while and come back, but. . .)

He had learned that *itte-kimasu* is used when the speaker wants to emphasize his intention of coming back, but had not used it himself and had not paid much attention to it before.

Then Mr. Takada said to Miss Yoshida

Ja, kono tegami-mo dashite-kite-moraeru?

(Then will you mail this letter for me? — *lit.* Then can I receive the favor of your mailing this letter too and then coming back?)

Mr. Lerner was surprised that Mr. Takada had used three, not two, verbs together — *dasu* (to mail), *kuru* (to come) and *morau* (to receive); he felt that if he had to learn this type of expression he really had a long way to go.

✳ ✳ ✳

Using two verbs together is very common in daily conversation, and being able to do so helps make one's Japanese more expressive. Such expressions as *itte-kimasu* are made up of two verbs; *iku* is used here as the main verb and *kuru* as the helping verb, although any verb can be used as the main one. While the main verb is used to indicate the action, the helping verb expresses the intention or the mental attitude of the speaker or the doer. For instance, when one says

Yonde-mimasu.
(I'll read it and see how it is.)

yomu refers to the action while *miru* is used to indicate the speaker's interest in the result of the action. In a similar way when one says

Osoku natte-shimatta.
(I was late.)

the use of *shimau* implies that the speaker regrets what he has done.

Such verbs as *morau*, *itadaku* (to receive), *ageru* (to give), *kureru* (to give me) and *kudasaru* (to give me) are added to other verbs to indicate the speaker's giving or receiving a favor from someone. Thus you will sometimes hear three verbs together as in *dashite-kite-morau* which Mr. Takada used or as in:

Yonde-mite-itadakemasu-ka.
よんでみていただけますか。

(Will you read this and see how it is? — *lit.* Can I receive the favor of your reading it and seeing?)

Ato-de kekkoo-desu-kara
あとで けっこうですから
(Because it's all right to do it later)

A few days ago Miss Yoshida asked Mr. Lerner to help her with her work. She said that it wouldn't take long, adding

Ato-de kekkoo-desu-kara.
あとで けっこうですから。
(*lit.* Because it's all right to do it later.)

Mr. Lerner understood that she had added this out of consideration in not wanting to inconvenience him, but he didn't quite understand why she had ended the sentence with *kara*.

This reminded him of Sensee telling him that Japanese often use *kara* when it does not mean "because." They will say something like

Ocha-ga hairimashita-kara doozo.
(Tea is ready. Please come and have some.)

If you translate this as "Because tea is ready, please come," it will sound strange. He also had heard Mr. Takada saying to Miss Yoshida

Ashita kaesu-kara sen-en kashite.
(*lit.* Because I'm going to return it tomorrow, lend me ¥1,000.)

*　　　*　　　*

Kara is used to give a reason just as "because" or "since" does, but the reason indicated by the phrase with *kara* does not necessarily concern a fact. In other words, *kara* in *Kane-ga nai-kara kaenai* (Because I don't have the money, I

32

can't buy it) concerns a factual reason. The reason for not being able to buy something is the fact that the speaker doesn't have enough money. But *kara* is also used to indicate the reason why the speaker wants to do something.

Ato-de kekkoo-desu-kara tetsudatte-ku-dasai.

can be paraphrased as "I know that you are busy and I feel I shouldn't trouble you, so I'm saying that you don't have to do it right now but that you can do it later. BECAUSE I'm being so considerate I think I can be allowed to ask you to help me." In short, *Ato-de kekkoo-desu-kara* is used to justify the speaker's making the request rather than to explain why the speaker wants someone to help him. In the same way, in Mr. Takada's sentence *Ashita kaesu-kara sen-en kashite*, *Ashita kaesu-kara* is said to justify his request.

Using *kara* is avoided when one should not openly justify oneself. For instance, when asked why you are late, it's more polite to say

Densha-ga okuremashita-node.
(Because the train was late.)

Node is used to objectively state a reason and is also used on more formal occasions. If you said

Densha-ga okuremashita-kara.

it would imply that you are asking to be spared criticism.

O-ari-desu-ka
おありですか
(Do you have it?)

Japanese pronunciation is not very difficult for Mr. Lerner, but aural comprehension is sometimes quite difficult. He had another embarrassing experience last Friday. Mr. Okada came and asked him if he would be free in the evening. Mr. Lerner thought that he had asked

O-shigoto-ga owari-desu-ka.
おしごとが　おわりですか。
(Will your work be finished? — *lit.* Is your work finished?)

so he answered yes. Then to his surprise Mr. Okada said that he was sorry and suggested that they go some other day. When Mr. Lerner said that he would prefer that evening, Mr. Okada looked puzzled.

The fact was that Mr. Okada had said

O-shigoto-ga o-ari-desu-ka.
おしごとが　おありですか。
(Do you have some work to do?)

and Mr. Lerner had answered yes.

*　　　*　　　*

The two expressions *o-ari-desu-ka* (do you have it?) and *owari-desu-ka* (is it finished?) sound very similar because the "w" sound in *owari* is pronounced lightly. The "w" sound in Japanese is pronounced softly and without much lip-rounding. Therefore foreigners often have difficulty distinguishing *wakai* (young) from *akai* (red) and *warawaremashita* (I was laughed at) from *arawaremashita* (it appeared).

The "r" sound is also difficult to hear, and misunderstanding can easily be caused by confusing *ri* with "i"; *karimashita* (I borrowed it) sounds similar to *kaimashita* (I bought it).

Not only the "w" and "r" sounds, but all Japanese consonants are usually pronounced more softly than those in English. This means that pronouncing the consonants softly will make your Japanese sound better. (And it is also important that while the consonants are pronounced softly, each of the vowels is pronounced clearly and with almost equal length.)

To see how softly Japanese consonants are pronounced, it may help to observe the way sales-girls in department stores talk to their customers. When they say

Maido arigatoo-gozaimasu.
(Thank you very much for your patronage.),

the "m" sound in *maido* and *gozaimasu* is pronounced very lightly. Especially when they pronounce the "m" in *gozaimasu*, sometimes their lips do not touch at all: in fact, their *gozaimasu* often sounds as if they are saying . . .*gozaiasu.*

Hajimemashite
はじめまして
(How do you do?)

The other day Mr. Lerner introduced one of his friends, Miss Winters, to Mr. Takada. When Mr. Lerner and Miss Winters arrived at the lobby of the hotel where they had arranged to meet, Mr. Takada was already there sitting on a sofa. He stood up when he saw them, and they walked over to him. When Mr. Lerner introduced him to Miss Winters, she stepped forward to him and said.

Hajimemashite, *Takada-san. Winters-desu.*
はじめまして
(How do you do, Mr. Takada? My name is Winters.)

just as Mr. Lerner had told her to do.

But a strange thing happened. Mr. Takada suddenly stepped back away from her and then said

Doozo yoroshiku.
どうぞ　よろしく。
(Glad to meet you.)

Miss Winters was not pleased by this. Later she said that she felt hurt at Mr. Takada's stepping back at the moment he saw her. Was she so frightening? Or did she look so unpleasant? No! Mr. Lerner denied her suspicions. In fact, she was a beautiful young woman, tall and well-built. But as someone who knew something about the Japanese, he thought he could understand why

36

Mr. Takada had stepped back. Japanese usually keep more distance between them when they talk than Americans do, and the distance is even greater when the two are speaking politely. For most Japanese it is embarrassing to stand too close to someone with whom they should talk politely. Mr. Takada, he emphasized, had stepped back not because he was afraid of her, or because he wanted to hurt her, but because he wanted to be perfectly correct.

*   *   *

When Mr. Lerner asked him if he was right, Sensee said he was. And Sensee added that probably the speaker-listener distance will vary depending on whether the two people bow or shake hands. When the two are going to bow to each other, they have to stand relatively far apart; if they are going to shake hands, they have to stand closer together. And among people bowing, too, the distance can vary according to the degree of bowing; the deeper the bow, the greater the distance.

Those who teach Japanese to foreigners often feel embarrassed when their students stand closer than they are expected to. This is especially true when the teacher and the student are of different sexes. In the same way, you may have experienced something awkward about shaking hands with a Japanese because he was standing far away from you.

In conversation, all expressions have to be said not only with the right grammar and right pronunciation, but also with the appropriate manner. This "manner" refers not only to body posture but also to the speaker-listener distance.

Mooshiwake arimasen
もうしわけ　ありません
(I'm very sorry)

A few weeks ago Mr. Lerner forgot to bring a book that Mr. Takada had asked him to bring. He felt sorry about it and said

Doomo sumimasen.
(I'm very sorry.)

And Mr. Takada said politely

Iie, ii-n-desu-yo.
(No, that's all right.)

but it was obvious that Mr. Lerner's negligence had inconvenienced him a great deal. So Mr. Lerner apologized again with a more polite expression

Hontoo-ni mooshiwake arimasen.
ほんとうに　もうしわけ　ありません。
(I'm very sorry. — *lit.* I really have no apology to offer.)

Then Miss Yoshida who happened to be with them suddenly started laughing. When Mr. Lerner asked her what was so funny, she said that although he had apologized with polite expressions the way he had said them did not sound at all as if he was sorry. In fact, she said, he looked like a soldier reporting his actions to an officer.

Mr. Lerner suspected that his pronunciation was poor, so when he met Sensee a few days later he asked him about it.

No, Sensee said, it was not the pronunciation, but the bodily expression that was wrong. Mr. Lerner had said *Mooshiwake arimasen* (I'm very sorry) with his upper body held upright and with his chin up. That is not the way a Japanese would apologize, even to his friends.

✻   ✻   ✻

Saying things in an inappropriate manner is not only ineffective but also likely to cause misunderstanding. Apologizing or making a request while standing straight and with the chin up will seem quite strange to the Japanese; it may even be offensive. A very fluent speaker of Japanese we know once experienced this kind of misunderstanding.

Japanese often bow or bend their upper body not only when apologizing or making a request but also when offering things. It is necessary to do so when offering sympathy to someone for his misfortune. You may have seen in person or in dramas how Japanese offer their condolences to a bereaved person. The set expression

Kono tabi-wa tonda koto-de gozaimashita.
(I'm very sorry to hear it. — *lit.* This time it was a terrible thing.)

is not said clearly to the end; usually people bow or look down saying just

Kono tabi-wa doomo. . .
(*lit.* This time indeed. . .)

and the rest is either mumbled or said inaudibly. In such cases bowing is as eloquent, or even more eloquent, than words.

Ikura-desu-ka
いくらですか
(How much is it?)

At a little souvenir shop Mr. Lerner saw a set of coasters which he thought would be good for his mother. So he asked the shopkeeper

Kore, ikura-desu-ka.
これ、いくらですか。
(How much is this?)

The shopkeeper, a man of about forty, came over to him and started explaining how carefully the coasters were made and what a bargain they were. He went on and on but never said how much they were.

Mr. Lerner felt uneasy. Though his question was a very simple one he might have said it wrong and caused a misunderstanding. He didn't want to know how well the coasters were made; he just wanted to know the price. But he wasn't sure that he could explain this in Japanese. He gave up and left the shop.

A few days later, he saw a tie that he liked in a store and wanted to know the price. Since it was displayed on a high shelf, he pointed to it and asked the woman at the shop

Are, o-ikura-deshoo-ka.
(How much would that be?)

trying to be very distinct and very polite. The woman bowed with a smile, and said

Arigatoo-gozaimasu.

(Thank you very much.)

*　　　*　　　*

When a person responds to another in Japan, the response may be towards the speaker's intention or wish rather than towards the verbal meaning of the question. For instance, when one asks someone *Samuku arimasen-ka* (Aren't you cold?), the answer to the verbal meaning of the question is either *Ee, samui-desu* or *Iie, samuku arimasen*. But if the listener takes the question as an indication of kindness, he will say something like *Arigatoo-gozaimasu* or *Doozo okamai-naku* (Please don't bother). If he thinks that the speaker is indirectly hinting that he himself is cold, he may say *Mado-o shimemashoo-ka* (Shall I close the window?)

In the same way, the shopkeepers in the above cases took Mr. Lerner's question *Ikura-desu-ka* as an indication of his intention to buy their merchandise and answered him accordingly.

In a model dialogue, the answer to the question *Ikura-desu-ka* must be . . . *en-desu*. At least language textbooks usually give this kind of dialogue. But in actual conversations, people do not always answer . . . *en-desu* when asked *Ikura-desu-ka*. In fact, in a survey made by a small group of researchers we know, people gave various other answers more often than . . . *en-desu*.

Therefore this was not because Mr. Lerner was a foreigner; a Japanese customer will have the same experience as well. But he won't be surprised or hurt. He may spend more time chatting with the shopkeeper and eventually find out the price instead of leaving immediately as Mr. Lerner did.

Otsukaresama-deshita
おつかれさまでした
(You must be tired)

Last Saturday Mr. Lerner went shopping at a large supermarket downtown. There he took the elevator to the second floor. When the elevator started going upward, the girl at the door said

Shooshoo omachi-kudasai.
(Please wait a little bit.)

So he expected that he would have to wait a while, but the elevator reached the second floor in less than a minute. Then the girl bowed and said

Omatase-itashimashita.
(I'm sorry I kept you waiting.)

Mr. Lerner didn't think he had waited long enough to receive such a polite apology. He guessed that it was because the Japanese are always in a hurry and hate being kept waiting even for a short time. At the cashier's too, he was told that she was sorry to have kept him waiting a long time, although he had not waited more than two minutes.

Afterwards he went to the barber's near his house. When the haircut was finished, the barber said, while taking the white cloth off from around his neck,

Otsukaresama-deshita.
おつかれさまでした。
(*lit.* You must be tired.)

42

Well, what Mr. Lerner had done was just sit in the chair and dream lazily about various things. He was not at all tired; he wanted to say that it was the barber himself that must have gotten tired. But before he could find the proper expression, the barber bowed and said

Shitsuree-itashimashita.
(*lit.* I'm sorry I was rude.)

＊　　　＊　　　＊

Mr. Lerner felt that he had been treated very kindly all that day. When he met Sensee in the evening he said jokingly that he felt as if he had become a very old man, short-tempered and easily tired. Sensee laughed and said that was the way Japanese like to thank others. They often apologize or show sympathy to express their thanks. For instance, a train conductor often adds *Otsukaresama-deshita* to *Maido gojoosha arigatoo-gozaimasu* (Thank you for riding our train). Actually *Otsukaresama-deshita* means "Thank you for your patience" or "Thank you for your patronage."

Sensee gave another instance. A comedian may thank his audience by saying

Gotaikutsusama-deshita which literally means "You must be bored."

Mr. Lerner wondered if he should conclude his Japanese compositions with *Gotaikutsusama-deshita* or *Otsukaresama-deshita* or a combination of the two, to thank Sensee for the patience with which he corrected them. Sensee laughed and waved his hands to show rejection of this idea.

Owasuremono-no nai yoo-ni
おわすれものの　ない　ように
(Please take care not to leave anything behind)

Last Saturday Mr. Lerner and Miss Winters took a train to go to a party at their friend's. When they reached the station and got off onto the platform, they heard an announcement from the loudspeaker

> *Owasuremono-no nai yoo-ni.*
> おわすれものの　ない　ように。

Miss Winters asked Mr. Lerner what it meant. He explained that it was a warning to the passengers not to leave anything behind on the train.

When they started going down the stairs, they again heard an announcement:

> *Oashimoto-ni gochuui-kudasai.*

Miss Winters, when she learned that this meant "Please watch out for the steps," looked down at the stairs and remarked that the announcement was not necessary because the stairs were not very steep nor particularly slippery.

After they got off the train they took a bus. When the bus was going to turn a corner, there was an announcement warning the passengers to watch out:

> *Yuremasu-kara gochuui-negaimasu.*
> (*lit.* Since the bus will rock, please be careful.)

Miss Winters wondered why Japanese like to warn others to behave correctly. A person of normal intelligence should know that he has to take care not to leave things behind, to fall on the stairs, or be thrown out of his seat when the bus suddenly turns a corner. Don't the Japanese feel annoyed or insulted when they are warned unnecessarily?

*   *   *

Mr. Lerner was reminded of the days when he started to realize what was being said around him; he had felt quite irritated just as Miss Winters did. But now he feels a little differently; he has come to take these warnings simply as a matter of course.

The Japanese feel they should show consideration for the people around them and passengers temporarily belong to the same group as the railroad employees. One must be as attentive as possible to others in the group so that they won't be in any discomfort or danger. Therefore many warnings are given to passengers, including such as:

Hakusen-no uchigawa-ni sagatte omachi-kudasai.

(Please wait for the train standing behind the white line on the platform.)

These warnings which may seem patronizing to foreigners are given, not because they think their passengers are careless or mentally retarded, but because they want them to be as safe as possible.

To yuu-to . . .
と いうと……
(So . . .?)

A few weeks ago Miss Yoshida asked Mr. Lerner if he would be able to come to a party at her house on Saturday. Mr. Lerner had made plans to go to Kyoto on that day, so he said,

Sono hi-wa ikemasen. **To yuu-to** *Kyooto-e ikanakereba narimasen.*

meaning "I won't be able to come on that day. The reason is that I must go to Kyoto." He had learned the expression *to yuu-to* which he understood is used before explaining what preceded. Miss Yoshida understood what he meant, but she said that *to yuu-to* somehow seemed strange.

Mr. Takada agreed with her and said that Mr. Lerner should have used *to yuu-no-wa* instead when stating the reason for what he had said. He added that *to yuu-to* is used when asking someone else to give a reason.

*　　*　　*

The two expressions are fundamentally used for different purposes. *To yuu-no-wa* (which literally means "To say . . . is") is used when giving the reason for the preceding statement. On the other hand *to yuu-to* (literally "when you say . . ." or "when I say . . .") is used to continue or develop the preceding statement; it corresponds to the English "so . . ." or "so . . .?"

But in actual usage these two expressions give quite different impressions. Suppose someone has said that he won't be able to come on a certain day and you want to know why. The following two conversations are both correct grammatically but there is some difference in politeness.

I. A: *Sono hi-wa korarenai-n-desu-ga.* (I won't be able to come on that day.)

    B: *To yuu-no-wa . . .?* と いうのは……？

    A: *Kyooto-e iku-n-desu.* (I'm going to Kyoto.)

II. A: *Sono hi-wa korarenai-n-desu-ga.*

    B: *To yuu-to . . .?* と いうと……？

    A: *Kyooto-e iku-n-desu.*

The speaker B may sound impolite in I. Since *to yuu-no-wa* is used to directly ask for the reason, it tends to sound demanding. In social situations it is usually replaced by *to yuu-to* even when one wishes to know the reason. And in this case *to iimasu-to* or *to osshaimasu-to* is used to sound more polite.

Saying *to yuu-no-wa . . .?* sounds like bluntly asking "Why?" as in a police detective examining a suspect or a teacher asking a student to prove the validity of his answer. It should be especially avoided when the question concerns something that the speaker may not want to talk about. And, to be more polite, one should just say *Soo-desu-ka* (Is that so?) or *Haa . . .* (Yes . . .?) and wait for the other to start giving the reason.

Okyakusan
おきゃくさん
(Visitor)

A few days ago Mr. Lerner dropped in at a little drugstore to buy something. When he was about to leave, the woman called out to him saying

Okyakusan, wasuremono-desu-yo.
(You've left something, sir.)

Mr. Lerner thanked her and picked up the package he had forgotten to take. He realized then that the word *okyakusan* which means "visitor" is used to refer to a customer, too.

On the following day, when he was waiting on the platform for the train, he heard a station employee address one of the passengers as *Okyakusan*. A passenger, he learned, is also called *okyakusan.* おきゃくさん。

Mr. Lerner wondered why the Japanese call a customer or passenger by the same name as a visitor; the latter does not involve payment while the former does. Then Sensee said that they all belong to the same category — someone who temporarily stays in the group. A customer is, in a sense, a visitor to a store and a passenger is a visitor to the railway company.

*   *   *

An *okyakusan* stays inside the group only for a limited time, and this fact results in how he is treated. Since he is not a member of the group in the strict sense, he is treated differently from the members. He is usually treated kindly and generously: the host will feed him with the best food he has; the *okyakusan* is asked to sit in the best seat and to take a bath first, etc. But he cannot fully participate in the activities of the group members. An *okyakusan* usually does not help wash the dishes after dinner, for instance; even if he offers to, the hostess will not let him.

Foreigners staying in Japan often feel that they are not accepted in Japanese groups and attribute this to their being foreigners. But Japanese themselves have a difficult time being accepted into a new group. In fact, an *okyakusan* is treated as such regardless of whether he is Japanese or a foreigner. Foreigners are treated differently mainly because they are *okyakusan* in Japanese society. This means that foreigners can be accepted as members of the group when they stop being regarded as *okyakusan*. That takes a long time and requires the satisfaction of various conditions depending on the nature of the group they want to get into. Thinking about a Japanese visitor hesitating at the entrance before stepping into a house may help you understand how an *okyakusan* is supposed to behave. The host will ask him to come into the house by saying

Doozo oagari-kudasai.
(Please come in.)

and the visitor will say

Demo, ojama-deshoo-kara. . .
(But I'd be disturbing you.)

After this is repeated a couple of times, the visitor will decide to "disturb" the family members. This is not a mere ceremony; it has to be done in order to show the *okyakusan*'s sincere respect for the group and to express his fear that he may disturb, rather than benefit, the group members by joining them.

Iie, honno sukoshi-de. . .
いいえ、ほんの すこしで……
(No, it's very little)

Mr. Lerner was invited to the Takadas last Saturday. When he arrived at their home, he saw Miss Yoshida, who had also been invited, handing a small package to her hostess. Mrs. Takada thanked her, admired the beautiful package, and asked

Ittai nan-deshoo-ne.
(I wonder what it can be.)

Then Miss Yoshida answered

Iie, honno sukoshi-de. . .
いいえ、ほんの すこしで……
(*lit.* No, it's very little.)

Mr. Lerner thought that this exchange was rather strange. When Mrs. Takada asked what the package contained, Miss Yoshida answered *iie*. She did not say what it was and Mrs. Takada did not ask again.

Mr. Lerner felt interested in this *iie*. People often say that the Japanese avoid saying *iie* to others, but sometimes they use *iie* when it does not seem necessary. The *iie* Miss Yoshida said would seem strange if directly translated into English as "No."

*   *   *

In Japan, people sometimes respond to the speaker's intention rather than to the literal meaning of what he has said. In other words, they try to find the intent behind what has ac-

50

tually been said, and respond to that intent. *Iie* in Japanese conversation is often used to deny what the speaker seems to expect. When Mrs. Takada asked what was inside the package, Miss Yoshida said *Iie*, meaning "I think you expect it to be something very good, but NO, you're wrong. It's nothing much." At the same time she also implied that Mrs. Takada did not have to feel obligated because the present was not much.

Thus *Iie* is often used to indicate one's modesty and consideration towards others. It is sometimes used simply to deny a compliment, but most often you will hear it used when someone has been asked to indicate his choice. For instance:

A: *Kore, itsu kaeseba ii-deshoo.* (When should I return this?)
B: *Iie, itsu-demo ii-n-desu-yo.* (*lit.* No, any time is OK.)
In this case, B's speech can be paraphrased as "No, you don't have to worry about returning it at some exact time. You can return it any time."
Or:
A: *Koohii-to koocha-to dochira-ga ii-deshoo.* (Which would you like, coffee or tea?)
B: *Iie, dotchi-demo.* (*lit.* No, either will do.)

This *Iie* is very often contracted and pronounced *Ie*; in men's familiar speech it is usually pronounced *Iya*. And this is followed quickly by the rest of the sentence without a long pause.

Sore-wa-desu-ne. . .

それはですね……

(That is, you know. . .)

Mr. Lerner has recently named Mr. Okada "Mr. *Desu-ne*" for one of his speech habits. Mr. Okada adds *desu-ne* to almost every phrase in his speech. For instance, when he wants to say that he had met Mr. Kobayashi in Shinjuku the day before, he will say:

Kinoo-desu-ne, Shinjuku-de-desu-ne, guuzen-desu-ne, Kobayashi-san-ni-desu-ne, aimashite-desu-ne. . .

(*lit.* Yesterday, you know, in Shinjuku, you know, I happened, you know, to meet Mr. Kobayashi, you know. . .)

Mr. Lerner doubts that Mr. Okada could speak at all if he were told not to use *desu-ne*. In English, *desu-ne* might be translated as "you know," but the use of "you know" is far less frequent, and not only that, its frequent use will be taken as a sign of poor speech. To Mr. Lerner, the Japanese seem to be much more permissive about this kind of speech habit. It is rather strange that they are tolerant towards such a habit while they are quite particular and meticulous about the level of politeness.

*　　　*　　　*

Sensee says that many Japanese will feel the same way as Mr. Lerner about the excessive use of *desu-ne*, and that Mr. Okada himself will try not to use it so much when the situation requires. But to a certain extent frequent use of *desu-ne* is usually tolerated in conversation. It is not only tolerated but also regarded as positively good in some situations, since it helps to add a friendly, relaxed tone.

Desu-ne is most often used when starting to explain something complicated. Before the explanation, the Japanese often say:

Sore-wa desu-ne. . .
それはですね……
(*lit.* That is, you know. . .)

in order to have the listener get ready.

Or, when one has to say something he doesn't want to, he naturally hesitates and says

Jitsu-wa-desu-ne. . .
(*lit.* The fact is, you know. . .)

In such cases the use of *desu-ne* between phrases is not regarded as a sign of poor speech; on the contrary, it is preferred to abruptly starting an explanation.

But the excessive use of *desu-ne* tends to disturb the development of a sentence and its end often has little to do with its start. Therefore *desu-ne* should be avoided when giving a clear explanation in which consistency is important. Just because of this, it can be used to mystify the listener or make him believe an illusion; a salesman or a politician often resorts to using *desu-ne* frequently when trying to persuade others.

Oishii-desu-ne, kono koohii
おいしいですね、このコーヒー
(It's good, this coffee)

A few weeks ago Mr. Lerner had a cup of coffee at a little coffee shop with Miss Yoshida. After tasting the coffee, Miss Yoshida remarked

Oishii-desu-ne, kono koohii.
おいしいですね、このコーヒー。
(*lit.* It's good, this coffee.)

He agreed, but thought to himself that he would have said *Kono koohii-wa oishii-desu-ne* without reversing the order of the subject and the predicate. When he asked her if she would like another cup, she said

Iie, juubun-desu, ippai-de.
(*lit.* No, it's enough, with one cup.)

reversing the order of the phrases again.

After that he paid special attention to the conversations around him, and noticed that this type of inversion is used very often. And he also realized that he himself had never done this; he wondered if he should sometimes try it when speaking Japanese.

* * *

In daily conversation the Japanese often reverse the order of the subject and the rest of the sentence, or start their sentences with what usually comes last. Strictly speaking, the word order does not change freely but the order of phrases can be changed; you can say *Oishii-desu-ne, kono koohii*, but you cannot say *Desu-ne oishii*,

54

koohii kono. In fact, you will often hear such sentences as:

> *Ii otenki-desu-ne, kyoo-wa.*
> (*lit.* It's a fine day, today.)
> *Yokatta-desu-ne, ano eega.*
> (*lit.* It was good, that movie.)
> *Kimashita-yo, henji-ga.*
> (*lit.* It came, the reply.)

By inversing the order in this way, you can give an impression of familiarity and enthusiasm. Because of this, inversion is most often used in speech that expresses one's emotions such as surprise, criticism, excitement, evaluation and the like. It is usually avoided in formal speech as well as in written language.

Foreigners may not feel it's correct to say sentences like *Oishii-desu-ne, kono koohii,* but they could first try such inversion as giving an explanation after the main sentence. For example, when one wants to say "Please wait a moment. I'll come in a minute," one can say either

> *Sugu modorimasu-kara matte-ite-kudasai.*
> (*lit.* Because I'm coming back in a minute, please wait.)
>   or
> *Chotto matte-ite-kudasai, sugu modorimasu-kara.*

Both are correct, but the second sentence sounds more conversational.

Moo sorosoro dekakenai-to. . .
もう　そろそろ　でかけないと……
(If we don't leave soon. . .)

Mr. Lerner invited the Takadas out to a movie last Saturday. When he reached their home, Mr. Takada was busy taking care of his plants in the garden. Mrs. Takada, all dressed up, went down to him and told him that it was time to go. But Mr. Takada was absorbed in his work. Then Mrs. Takada said

Moo sorosoro dekakenai-to. . .
もう　そろそろ　でかけないと……
(*lit.* If we don't slowly go out now. . .)

So Mr. Takada got ready and the three of them went out together.

When the movie was over Mr. Takada suggested having tea together, but Mrs. Takada said

Demo, amari osoku naru-to. . .
(*lit.* But if it gets too late. . .)

After parting from the Takadas Mr. Lerner recalled Mrs. Takada's two sentences and noticed that they were not complete ones. And he realized that he had heard many such incomplete sentences spoken by Japanese.

*　　*　　*

Sensee said that Mrs. Takada's sentences were complete sentences in the sense that they conveyed their meanings perfectly well without adding any other phrases. The first sentence meant "We should go now" and the second one "We shouldn't stay too late." Each of them can be followed, as far as the stated meaning is concerned, by a phrase indicating what will result, but the addition will change the implied meaning. If she had said *Moo sorosoro dekakenai-to osoku narimasu*, (*lit.* If we don't slowly start now, we'll be late), it would have sounded more demanding or as if she were criticizing her husband. A similar thing can be said of the second sentence *Amari osoku naru-to.* . . Probably she meant that if they stayed too late they would take too much of Mr. Lerner's time or cause some other inconvenience. But if she had said that out loud, it might have embarrassed Mr. Lerner. Thus she purposely chose to end her sentences with . . *to* because of her reserve.

Similarly, . . *tara* is used when suggesting that others do something. For instance, instead of saying *Moo sorosoro dekakenai-to.* . . you can say *Moo sorosoro dekaketara.* . . (*lit.* If you slowly go out now. . .) without adding the phrase that usually follows, *doo-desu-ka* (how is it?), meaning "Why don't you go out now?" This is more direct than *dekakenai-to.* . . This is so because *doo-desu-ka* or a similar phrase is always implied after . . *tara*, while after . . *to* various statements can be implied, thus leaving more to the listener to interpret for himself.

You will often hear sentences ending in . . *to*, . . *tara*, and the like, especially in reserved speech. Leaving the concluding part unsaid in this way is not a sign of poor speaking, but is rather regarded as positively good because it shows consideration towards others.

Sayoonara
さようなら
(Good-bye)

Mr. Mori, director of the company where Mr. Lerner works, said when leaving the office the other day.

Ja, kyoo-wa kore-de.
(*lit.* Then, today, with this.)

So Mr. Lerner said *Sayoonara* (Good-bye). But all the others who were there said something else. Mr. Lerner could not make out what they had said because several of them spoke at the same time, but it was clear that none of the expressions they used was *Sayoonara*. After that he paid special attention to the expressions used when parting, and found that *Sayoonara* is not used as often as he had expected.

*   *   *

Many people think that *Sayoonara* is the most typical expression used when parting, but there are several other expressions used as often, depending upon the situation. In fact, the use of *Sayoonara* or *Sayonara* is surprisingly limited.

Sayoonara is not used among family members, for one thing. When one leaves his home he says

Itte-kimasu or *Itte-mairimasu.*
いってきます。 いってまいります。
(*lit.* I will go and come back — *mairimasu* is more polite than *kimasu*.)

And the person remaining home says

Itte-(i)rasshai.
(*lit.* Please go and come back.)

Sayoonara is used between young people and to younger people, but not to older people or to one's superiors. When parting from one's elders or superiors one should say *Shitsuree-shimasu* (*lit.* I'm going to be rude) or some other polite expression. Some young people use *Sayoonara* indiscriminately to anyone regardless of age or position, but this is not considered good usage even though it is sometimes tolerated. College graduates who have just started working usually have a hard time getting rid of this kind of speech habit.

The teacher of Japanese to foreigners will often feel embarrassed when his adult students say to him *Sayoonara* or *Sensee, sayoonara* because it reminds him of schoolboys or schoolgirls saying good-bye to their teacher.

It is all right to use *Sayoonara* between friends or colleagues, but many people choose other familiar expressions, probably because *Sayoonara* can sound somewhat childish or remind people of their school days. Thus people say *Ja, kore-de*, *Ja, mata* (*lit.* Then, again) or *Ja. . .* (*lit.* Then. . .) when parting from their friends or colleagues. And to a person remaining at the office, they usually say *Osaki-ni*, meaning "I'm leaving before you."

Nan-to iimasuka
なんと いいますか
(What shall I say?)

A few days ago Mr. Okada was explaining his plan to Mr. Lerner and several others. When he came to a rather complicated part, he paused for a moment and said.

Nan-to iimasu-ka.
なんと いいますか。
(*lit.* What do you call it or What shall I say?)

Mr. Lerner thought that Mr. Okada was asking his listeners a question, but he didn't know what it was about, so he asked Mr. Okada *Nan-no koto-desu-ka* (What is it about?). But just at that moment Mr. Okada resumed his explanation, completely ignoring Mr. Lerner's question. Later Mr. Takada explained that the *Nan-to iimasu-ka* that Mr. Okada had said was not a question but actually a kind of stopgap phrase similar to the English "er. . ." or "you know. . .," so nobody had to answer him.

*　　　*　　　*

Nan-to iimasu-ka is used to indicate that the speaker is looking for the right expression. There are several other words and phrases used for this purpose; *anoo*, *sonoo*, *konoo* and *eeto* are used very often. Sometimes the prolonged vowel of the preceding word is used as in *Sore-wa aaa. . . .* (Care should be taken not to use English pause sounds such as "er. . ." or "uh. . ." but only Japanese vowels instead.)

But *nan-to iimasu-ka* is somewhat different from other expressions of this kind. Since it is said half to the speaker himself in a monologue-like way, it is not exactly a question. It actually means "I don't know how I should put this but let me try." When the speaker says this, he is indirectly asking the listener to join him in his search for the right word. It can be taken as a sign of uncertainty, but it can also be taken as consideration towards the listener; many Japanese seem to take the latter view and welcome the appropriate use of this expression as an indication of modesty.

This expression has several variants which are used depending upon the level of politeness; when compared with *nan-to iimasu-ka*, *nan-to mooshimasu-ka* is more polite and *nan-to iimashooka* sounds softer; *nan-to yuu-ka* is less polite and in very familiar speech *nan-te yuu-kana* is also used.

At any level of politeness, it must be said softly, fading out towards the end, and with a dangling intonation so that it won't be taken as a direct question.

Mooshiwake arimasen-ga, anoo. . .
もうしわけ　ありませんが、あのう……
(I'm very sorry, but. . .)

The other day Mr. Lerner and Mr. Takada went to Mr. Okada's office to discuss some business with him. After the discussion was over, Mr. Okada retained them and continued talking. To Mr. Lerner it seemed as if he were going to talk forever, and he felt irritated because he was rather busy that day. But he thought he should wait for Mr. Takada to say something, and suppressed his irritation.

When the talk seemed to have come to an end and there was a slight pause, Mr. Takada said

> *Mooshiwake arimasen-ga, anoo. . .*
> もうしわけ　ありませんが、あのう……
> (*lit.* I have no excuse to offer, but I. . .)

Then Mr. Okada quickly changed his tone and apologized for keeping them too long. Mr. Takada thanked him for spending so much time with them, in which Mr. Lerner joined. When the two stood up and were about to leave, Mr. Takada added casually

> *Mada sukoshi shigoto-ga arimasu-node. . .*
> (We have a little more work to do, so. . .)

*　　　*　　　*

Mr. Lerner was interested in the way Mr. Takada took his leave, so he asked Sensee if this was typically Japanese.

Sensee said it is. It is typically Japanese in many ways. First, Mr. Takada waited patiently

62

until there was a pause that showed the termination of one topic. In discussing business with Japanese, you usually have to be prepared to spend some time before and after the discussion itself.

Second, he just said that he was sorry and didn't say anything about his having to leave. Mr. Lerner would have said something like

Shigoto-ga arimasu-kara kaeranakereba narimasen
(Since I have some work to do, I have to leave.)

but Mr. Takada didn't say this. And Mr. Okada immediately took the hint and helped the guests get ready to say good-bye.

Very often a Japanese conversation will proceed without the speaker mentioning his desires and the listener makes an effort to understand these unspoken desires. A teacher of Japanese to foreigners will often feel embarrassed when he hears his students say something like

Moo ikanakereba narimasen.
(I have to go now.)

when leaving. This sentence is grammatically correct and the speaker means well, but actually Japanese do not usually speak so directly in this kind of situation. To the Japanese ear, this sounds as if the speaker is unnecessarily asserting himself; it can seem either rude or strangely dramatic.

Okuni-wa dochira-desu-ka
おくには　どちらですか
(What country is he from?)

The other day Miss Yoshida introduced Mr.
Lerner to her acquaintance, Mrs. Iwasaki. When
Mr. Lerner and Mrs. Iwasaki had exchanged
Hajimemashite (Glad to meet you) and *Doozo
yoroshiku* (How do you do?) and the three had
sat down to talk, Mrs. Iwasaki asked

> *Okuni-wa dochira-desu-ka.*
> おくには　どちらですか。
> (*lit.* Which way is the country?)

This could mean either "What country are you
from?" or "What country is he from?" From the
direction in which Mrs. Iwasaki posed this question, it was not clear whether she was asking
Miss Yoshida or Mr. Lerner. While Mr. Lerner
was wondering about this, Miss Yoshida answered the question. She answered the next several questions too, although they concerned Mr.
Lerner. He felt as if he were a little child taken
by his mother to an old friend of hers.
　It was rather unpleasant; did the two women
think his Japanese was so poor that he could not
join the conversation? He started thinking about
something else. Then all of a sudden, he realized
that Miss Yoshida had stopped answering Mrs.
Iwasaki's questions and was waiting for him to
answer. Did they realize that he was unhappy
about being ignored?

＊　　　＊　　　＊

　This custom is rather common in Japan, and
is not limited to conversations with a foreigner.

Miss Yoshida answered for him not because Mr. Lerner is a foreigner but because it is customary.

Suppose Mr. Lerner took Miss Yoshida to one of his Japanese acquaintances — Mr. Takahashi, his landlord, for instance. Mr. Takahashi would want to know about Miss Yoshida and ask such questions as

Otsutome-desu-ka.
(Are you working? or Is she working?)

And Miss Yoshida would not answer as readily as she had answered Mrs. Iwasaki's questions when she took him to her, but would wait for Mr. Lerner to answer for her. After a while, when Mr. Lerner stopped answering for her, she would start answering Mr. Takahashi for herself.

What underlies this custom seems to be respect towards the older members of the group. It can be simplified as follows: A and B have been acquaintances or friends for some time; A introduces C to B; then comes conversation between older member A and B first, while the member C waits until he is fully admitted into the group. Except when a question is clearly directed to C, at the beginning he refrains from answering B's questions. (Actually most of the questions about C can be taken either as being in the second or third person, but C usually waits for A to answer them.) As a rule, A's existence should not be ignored or neglected by the introduction of C.

And this is applied to situations where human relations matter most; it may not apply to emergencies or cases where business is given priority.

From Mr. Lerner's Diary

Mr. Lerner's diary mostly concerns usage of Japanese and might be called Nihongo Diary. With his permission, we'd like to show you some excerpts from it.

*   *   *

June 16, Friday
I made a funny mistake again today. While I was walking along the street, I wanted to know what time it was. I had left my watch at home, so I asked Mr. Takada, who was with me,

Jikan-ga arimasu-ka.

meaning "Do you have the time?" Then he asked me

Itsu? Konban? (When? This evening?)

I had forgotten that *Jikan-ga arimasu-ka* is usually used when asking someone to spend some time together. Mr. Takada warned me that I shouldn't say this to a young woman I happened to meet on the street or on the train. Instead, I should say

Sumimasen, ima nanji-deshoo-ka.
すみません、なんじでしょうか。
(Excuse me, what time is it now?)

*   *   *

June 23, Friday
Yesterday afternoon I heard that Mr. Okada's son had passed the examination to get into a very famous university, so I wanted to tell

Miss Yoshida about it first thing this morning. I said

Yoshio-san-wa shiken-o torimashita.

But Miss Yoshida didn't look impressed at all. She asked me if *shiken-o torimashita* was the literal translation of "he took an exam." She said I should have said

Shiken-ni toorimashita.
しけんに　とおりました。

to mean "he passed the examination." I had made two mistakes. One is that I pronounced the *too* sound of *toorimashita* too short; and I used the particle *o* instead of *ni*.

Then I remembered that I had once said *shiken-o moraimashita* to mean "I took an examination." Miss Yoshida corrected this and told me *morau* should be used only when receiving something good; it should be used with such things as *okane* (money), *okurimono* (present), and *oyomesan* (bride). I somewhat doubt the last one, but I thought this was a good explanation.

But Mr. Takada disagreed and said that *morau* should be used for something concrete; it is correct to say *shiken-no kami-o morau* to mean "to be given a test paper."

Hai, orimasen

はい、おりません

(Yes, he's not here)

A few weeks ago Mr. Lerner called Mr. Okada at his office. Miss Hayashi, his secretary, answered the phone. When Mr. Lerner asked

Okada-san, irasshaimasu-ka.
(Is Mr. Okada there?),

she answered

Hai, orimasen.
はい、おりません。
(*lit.* Yes, he's not here.)

Mr. Lerner thought this was strange. If he had asked *Okada-san, irasshaimasen-ka* (Isn't Mr. Okada there?), the answer could have been *Hai* because it is used to show agreement whether the answer is in the affirmative or negative. But in this case Mr. Lerner asked if Mr. Okada was there; why did Miss Hayashi say *Hai, orimasen*?

Later he asked Miss Yoshida if it was possible to say *Iie, orimasen* (No, he isn't here). She said it was. What a strange language Japanese is, to use either yes or no for the same purpose!

*   *   *

Hai is not the exact equivalent of the English "yes." It is essentially used to show the speaker's willingness to help or to obey. In Japanese conversation the listener often says *hai* when the speaker pauses, to show that he is listening attentively. This is called *aizuchi*. In this case *hai* does not necessarily indicate agreement with the speaker's statement; it simply means "I have heard you and am willing to listen." In the same way, what Miss Hayashi said can be paraphrased as "I have heard you, and am willing to help you. To help you, I will answer your question. My answer is that Mr. Okada is not here. What can I do for you?"

It is possible to say *lie, orimasen* instead. In that case she would be simply answering the question in the negative; she would not be showing any willingness to help. (It would be different if she said *lie, orimasen-ga . . .* or *lie, orimasen-kedo . . .*)

In a similar way *hai* can be used as in the next example:

A: *Okane, tariru-deshoo-ka.* (Do you think you have enough money?)
B: *Hai, chotto tarinai-kamo shiremasen.* (*lit.* Yes, it may be a little insufficient.)

B's answer actually means "Thank you for asking. I'm afraid I don't have enough."

Hai is also used to mean "Here you are," when handing something over to others. This can also be interpreted as an indication of willingness to help.

Wakarimashita-ka
わかりましたか
(Did you understand?)

A few weeks ago Mr. Lerner was explaining his proposal in Japanese to several people including the director, Mr. Mori, and Mr. Takada. When he had finished explaining the first part, he felt uncertain about whether or not his listeners had understood him, so he asked

Wakarimashita-ka.
わかりましたか。
(Did you understand?)

Mr. Takada smiled in the way that he did when he noticed one of Mr. Lerner's mistakes in Japanese, and said *Ee, wakarimashita*, but Mr. Mori remained silent, looking rather displeased. Mr. Lerner thought that he had not been polite enough, so he said *owakari-ni narimashita-ka*, choosing a more polite phrasing, but it didn't seem to work.

＊　　　　＊　　　　＊

It is natural for the speaker to want to make sure that the listener has understood him properly; this is especially true when the speaker is using a foreign language. In English, the speaker will use such expressions as "Did you understand?" "Did you get me?" "I hope you understood," or "I hope my explanation has been clear so far," depending on the situation.

In Japanese also, there are a variety of expressions and you have to be careful to choose the right one when you want to be polite. *Wakarimashita-ka* or *Wakarimasu-ka* (Do you understand?) should be avoided when talking to one's superiors. It would sound as if you were talking to a younger person or to a student. This is because the verb *wakaru* implies a person's mental ability; it sounds impolite to question someone's ability to understand even if the speaker means that his own explanation was not lucid enough. Using polite phrasing such as *owakari-ni narima-shita-ka* would make little difference.

Instead, in polite speech, the speaker has to resort to various indirect expressions to check the listener's understanding.

Yoroshii-deshoo-ka (Is it all right?)
or
Tsugi-e itte-mo yoroshii-deshoo-ka
(Is it all right to go on to the next part?)

is often used for this purpose.

Another method is to stimulate the listener's reaction by throwing out some dangling statement such as *Soo yuu wake-na-n-desu-ga* . . . (Such is the situation and . . .) or *Soo yuu koto-de* . . . (Such is the fact and . . .). Then the listener will usually say that he has understood so far and wants to hear more.

The idea is that the speaker should ask the listener if it is all right to go on rather than trying to directly check the listener's understanding.

Tanoshii hito
たのしい　人
(A happy person?)

Mr. Lerner was having coffee with Miss Yoshida and Mr. Takada during his break a few days ago. Miss Yoshida started talking about Mr. Kobayashi, a new colleague, and Mr. Takada commented on him saying

Ano hito, totemo tanoshii hito-desu-ne.
あの人、とても　たのしい　人ですね。

Mr. Lerner took it as "He's a very happy person," so he asked what made him so happy. The two didn't understand and looked at each other. After a while Miss Yoshida explained that Mr. Kobayashi was a good joker and always tried to make others laugh so she enjoyed talking with him. Mr. Lerner realized that *tanoshii hito* should be translated as "a person I am happy to associate with" or "an enjoyable person" rather than "a happy person."

*　　*　　*

Japanese adjectives for indicating emotions such as *tanoshii*, and *kanashii* (sad) are usually used to refer to the emotions of the speaker himself; one must use different expressions when referring to those of other persons. *Kanashii-desu* usually means "I'm sad," and *Kanashinde-imasu* or *Kanashigatte-imasu* is used to mean "He (or She) is sad." Or sometimes *Kanashisoo-desu* (He looks sad) is used. But *Kanashii hito-desu* is not usually used.

In a similar way, *taikutsuna hito* means "a boring person" rather than "a bored person."

Omoshiroi hito is an interesting person and not an interested person. (Incidentally, *omoshiroi* is not as positive as the English "interesting"; *omoshiroi eega* (interesting movie) is all right, but it is not proper to say something like *omoshiroi hito* or *omoshiroi koogi* (interesting lecture) about one's superiors.)

Some verbs ending in their -*ta* or -*da* form are not only used to indicate the past tense but also as modifiers. Among these expressions some are used in a similar way to *tanoshii hito*. *Odoroita hito* can mean "someone at whom I'm surprised" as well as "someone who is surprised." When someone says *Ano hito, odoroita hito-da*, he usually means "I'm really surprised at him." *Komatta hito* often means "someone who troubles me." You will often hear people talking about someone as

Komatta hito-desu-ne.
こまった 人ですね。
(He's such a bother.)

Doose watashi-wa . . .
どうせ　わたしは……
(After all I . . .)

The other day Mr. Takada praised Mr. Lerner's progress in Japanese and added that many Japanese study English at college but they don't speak English well. Then Miss Yoshida who was with them suddenly turned to Mr. Takada and said

Doose watashi-wa heta-desu-yo.
どうせ　わたしは　へたですよ。
(*lit.* After all I'm poor at it.)

Mr. Takada hastened to explain that he hadn't been referring to her at all, and she understood. Then someone there teased her by saying that it had been quite a while since he had last heard her use the word *doose*.

Mr. Lerner wanted to know what particular implications this word has, but the coffee break had come to an end. He later consulted a dictionary. It gave so many definitions — anyway, after all, as a matter of course, at all, etc. — that he found himself even more confused.

＊　　　＊　　　＊

Doose means "whatever one may do, the limit is already known and one cannot expect much." It is often used in a negative sense, and using it implies that the speaker is unhappily resigned. When Miss Yoshida said *Doose watashi-wa heta-desu-yo*, she meant "Since I am not bright, I can never be good at it."

Doose is different from *yappari* or *kekkyoku* in that it is used to indicate the speaker's expectation or judgment, and not to describe a fact. You can say *Yappari* (or *Kekkyoku*) *ma-ni aima-sen-deshita* (After all I couldn't get there in time), but one cannot say *Doose ma-ni aimasen-deshita*. On the other hand *Doose ma-ni aimasen-yo* (You won't be able to get there in time) is correct and, in fact, is often said to a person who is hurrying to a bus stop, for instance.

When a parent says *Kodomo-wa doose oya-kara hanarete-iku-n-desu*, it means "After all, children will leave their parents," implying that the parents should be prepared for that day.

Sensee remembers that there used to be many popular songs including this word when he was young. People used to like songs about lost love or lost happiness, and the lyrics of those songs contained such phrases as *doose watashi-wa* or *doose kono yo-wa* (*lit.* after all this world is. . .) Also, when women were supposed to be weak, such expression as *doose watashi-wa onna-da-kara* (I cannot do much because I am a woman — *lit.* Since I am a woman) were often heard.

Mr. Lerner tried to make up several sentences including this word; the one Sensee praised was

Doose gaijin-da-kara wakarimasen.
(Since I am a foreigner, I can never understand.)

although Sensee strongly opposed this idea.

Ocha-ga hairimashita-kedo. . .
お茶が　はいりましたけど……
(The tea is ready, but. . .)

A few weeks ago while Mr. Lerner was working at the office, Miss Yoshida came in and asked him to come over to the tea table saying

Ocha-ga hairimashita-kara. . .
(*lit.* Because the tea is ready,. . .)

Mr. Lerner understood that she wanted him to come for his tea, although she did not verbally say so. Japanese usually do not say *nonde-kudasai* (please drink it) or *nomi-ni kite-kudasai* (please come to drink it) after *Ocha-ga hairimashita* (The tea is ready).

The next day, when Mr. Lerner went to see Mr. Okada at his office, Miss Hayashi, his secretary, said to them

Ocha-ga hairimashita-kedo. . .
お茶が　はいりましたけど……
(*lit.* The tea is ready, but. . .)

implying that she wanted them to come to where the tea was served.

Since Mr. Lerner was paying special attention to how Japanese end their sentences, he noticed that the two women had used different sentence endings, *kara* (because) and *kedo* (but), in similar situations. To him these two seem so apart from each other in meaning that he can't understand how they can be used for the same purpose.

*　　　*　　　*

76

Kara and *kedo* are used with quite different meanings in factual statements, as in the following examples:

Ame-ga furimashita-kara ikimasen-deshita.
(Because it rained we didn't go.)
Ame-ga furimashita-kedo ikimashita.
(It rained but we went.)

But in making requests or asking about someone else's wishes, *kara* and *kedo* seem to be used in a similar way. Both *Ocha-ga hairimashita-kara* and *Ocha-ga hairimashita-kedo* can precede *doozo kite-kudasai* (please come), although this is usually left out. The two endings, however, reflect different attitudes on the part of the speaker. When he says . . .*kara*, he is asking someone to do him a favor as a matter of course, On the other hand, if he says . . .*kedo*, it shows that he is hesitant about making the request; in this case *kedo* can be paraphrased as ''I know I shouldn't trouble you, but.'' Thus, generally speaking, sentences ending in . . .*kedo* sound more polite than those ending in . . .*kara*.

You can urge someone to start something either by saying

Moo jikan-desu-kara. . . (Because it's already time,. . .)
    or
Moo jikan-desu-kedo. . . (It's already time, but. . .)

The latter sounds more polite and is usually preferred.

(*Keredomo* and *keredo* are sometimes used in place of *kedo* without changing the meaning; *kedo* is more conversational and familiar.)

From Mr. Lerner's Diary

Aug. 1, Tuesday
What a hot day it was today! When I arrived at the office at nine, I was quite tired and didn't feel like working. So I said to Miss Yoshida

Kyoo-wa daibu atatakai-desu-ne.

meaning it was very warm. She didn't immediately agree; she smiled and said that I had a good sense of humor. No, it wasn't a question of humor but one of heat and humidity.

Sensee explained that *atatakai* in Japanese is always used in a good sense; it should be translated as ''nice and warm'' rather than just ''warm'' when referring to the weather. Thus *daibu atatakai* is a proper expression when used in some other season, such as early spring when people are happy about the end of the cold weather. On such a hot morning as this, I should have said just *Atsui-desu-ne!* あついですね。

*　　　*　　　*

Aug. 3, Thursday
What recently bothers me about the Japanese is that they use the ''t'' sound so often in rapid speech. Today I said

Watashi-ga itatte dame-desu.

meaning ''What I say won't work'' (*lit.* Even if I say it, it will be no good), but nobody understood. Miss Yoshida, who is always quick at understanding me, corrected me and said *Watashi-ga ittatte.*

Itatte means ''even if I exist,'' while *ittatte*

78

means "even if I say." Using the "t" sound three times instead of four makes a big difference in meaning. In the same way,

kitatte きたって means "even if I wear it" or "even if I come" while
kittatte きったって means "even if I cut it."
And shitatte したって means "even if I do" while shittatte しったって means "even if I know."

When I was practicing these phrases, Mr. Takada appreciated my effort and said that pronunciation counts so much in language learning. He emphasized it by saying

Nantettatte.

I later learned that this is the contraction of nanto ittatte (whatever one may say). Five t's in such a short phrase —

Nantettatte nihongo-wa muzukashii!
(No matter what you may say, Japanese is a difficult language.)

Kekkon-suru koto-ni narimashita

けっこんする　ことに　なりました

(It's been decided that we are going to get married)

Last Sunday afternoon while Mr. Lerner was watching TV at home, someone rang the doorbell. It was Mr. Fukuda, his colleague, standing side by side with a young woman whom Mr. Lerner had seen with him a few times. Mr. Fukuda introduced her and said

Boku-tachi, kekkon-suru koto-ni narimashita.
ぼくたち、けっこんする　ことに　なりました。
(*lit.* It's been decided that we are going to get married.)

Mr. Lerner congratulated them and asked them to come in, but they declined; they were apparently on a busy tour of marriage announcements.

After they left, Mr. Lerner thought about the expression *kekkon-suru koto-ni narimashita.* He had once learned that . . . *koto-ni naru* means "doing something is decided upon, . . . *koto-ni suru* means "to decide on doing something." Getting married should be a matter of the will of the two people involved; why did Mr. Fukuda say . . . *koto-ni narimashita*? Are some young Japanese still so feudalistic about marriage?

＊　　　＊　　　＊

. . . *suru* refers to an intentional action while *naru* refers to some unintentional action. When one decides to go to a movie, he usually says *Eega-o mi-ni iku koto-ni shimashita* (I decided to go to a movie). When one decides not to buy something, he says *Kawanai koto-ni shimashita* (I

80

decided not to buy it). On the other hand, when a company employee is ordered to go abroad, for instance, he says *Furansu-e iku koto-ni narima-shita* (It's been decided that I go to France).

. . . *koto-ni naru* is also used when the speaker doesn't know, or doesn't want to tell, who has made the decision, and it often implies that the decision has been made not by a mere individual but either by the public or by some authoritative power. Because of this, a store owner telling the customer about a rise in price usually says *neage-suru koto-ni narimashita* (it's been decided the price be raised) instead of *neage-suru koto-ni shimashita* (I decided to raise the price).

In announcing one's marriage too, one sometimes chooses *kekkon-suru koto-ni naru* because it implies that the decision has been made by the will of everybody, not by the two involved alone. This expression is used most in formal situations rather than in familiar conversations between family members or close friends. If one said *kek-kon-suru koto-ni shimashita* in a formal situation, it would sound either immature or as if the two were getting married in defiance of the people around them.

Kyoo-wa kin'yoobi-deshita-ne

きょうは　金曜日でしたね

(Today was Friday, wasn't it?)

Mr. Lerner was having beer with Mr. Okada and Mr. Takada last Friday evening. During their friendly conversation, Mr. Okada asked Mr. Lerner

Raanaa-san-niwa imooto-san-ga arimashita-ne.
(*lit.* There was a younger sister to Mr. Lerner, wasn't there?, or, You had a sister, Mr. Lerner, didn't you?)

Mr. Lerner was so shocked by the phrase *arimashita* (there was) that he couldn't speak for a moment. Why did Mr. Okada use the past tense to refer to his sister as if she were no longer alive? But Mr. Okada looked very casual and Mr. Takada told him that Mr. Lerner has a sister named Margaret. Then Mr. Okada asked again

Oikutsu-deshita-ka.
(*lit.* How old was she?)

Mr. Lerner thought that he should use the same form although he didn't understand why the past form should be used, so he said *Juuhachi-deshita* (She was 18). This time Mr. Okada looked surprised, and Mr. Takada asked Mr. Lerner why he had answered *Juuhachi-deshita* instead of *Juuhachi-desu* (She is 18). Mr. Takada even mumbled something about a terrible possibility — her death!

* * *

Japanese use the past tense when they want to confirm information they acquired in the past. Thus they often say something like

Kyoo-wa kin'yoobi-deshita-ne.
きょうは　金曜日でしたね。
(Today's Friday, isn't it? — *lit.* Today was Friday, wasn't it?)
　or
Ano-hito, megane-o kakete-imashita-ne.
(He wears glasses, doesn't he? —*lit.* He was wearing glasses, wasn't he?)

when they are not sure about their memory.

In a similar way, when they meet someone whose name they cannot recall, they say

Shitsuree-desu-ga, donata-deshita-ka.
(Excuse me, but who are you? —*lit.* I am rude, but who were you?)

If they say *donata-desu-ka* instead of *donata-deshita-ka*, it means that they have not seen the person before.

Sometimes *-kke* is added to the past form to make it clearer that the speaker wants to confirm his memory. Thus:

Kyoo-wa kin'yoobi-deshita-kke.
(Today's Friday, right?)
Donata-deshita-kke.
(I forgot who you are although I have met you.)

O-isha-san-no o-kage-de. . .

おいしゃさんの　おかげで……

(Thanks to the doctor. . .)

Mr. Lerner read in a book recently that men should be careful not to use feminine expressions when speaking Japanese. Using "*o*" with nouns is a sign of feminine speech, for instance. So he decided to avoid using it whenever possible. Yesterday morning, when Mr. Takada asked him if he had recovered from his cold, he answered

Isha-san-no kage-de yoku narimashita.

meaning "I'm better thanks to the doctor." He had been saying *o-isha-san* for "doctor" and *o-kage-de* to mean "thanks to," but this time he left out the "*o*" for both of them. He thought he sounded more masculine this way, but Mr. Takada laughed a lot. He said *kage-de* means "behind someone's back," so Mr. Lerner's sentence meant "I became better behind the doctor's back." And one more correction is needed; people usually say *o-isha-san*, not *isha-san*.

O-isha-san-no o-kage-de. . .
おいしゃさんの　おかげで……

*　　　*　　　*

One purpose of adding "*o*" to various words is to show respect to others. For instance, to mean "Are you well?" it is more polite to say *O-genki-desu-ka* than to say *Genki-desu-ka*. This "*o*" is also added to words referring to the belongings of others as in *o-kuruma* (your car) and *o-taku* (your house).

Another purpose of adding it is to make the

tone of speech more polite. It is often added to things or people that do not need to be referred to with respect. For instance, *o-sake* or *o-kane* is used even when referring to *sake* or money that does not belong to anyone. Women use this "*o*" more often than men; women almost always say *o-sake* or *o-kane* while men say either *o-sake* or *sake* depending on the situation.

Sometimes both "*o*" and "*san*" are added together to the name of a person or an occupation in order to show respect. Doctors are usually called *o-isha-san* instead of *isha-san*; this applies to *kyaku* (visitor), too.

Since "*o*" shows a positive evaluation, it cannot be added to such words as *doroboo* (thief) or *kichigai* (insane person). It is not usually added to loan words from other languages, either; you cannot add it to TV or radio and say *o-terebi* or *o-rajio*. This is not because the Japanese do not appreciate TV or radio but because these words are newcomers to Japanese vocabulary and have not yet been accepted as its regular members.

Itsumo nikoniko shite-imasu
いつも にこにこ しています
(She always has a nice smile)

While Mr. Lerner, Mr. Takada and Mr. Okada were chatting leisurely for a while after their business discussion, Mr. Okada mentioned that Miss Yoshida was a very pleasant woman. Mr. Lerner heartily agreed with him so he said

Itsumo nitanita shite-imasu-ne.

meaning "She always has a nice smile." But Mr. Okada looked embarrassed and Mr. Takada burst out laughing. After a while Mr. Takada stopped laughing and explained that Mr. Lerner should have said

Itsumo nikoniko shite-imasu-ne.
いつも にこにこ していますね。

Mr. Lerner realized that he had made a mistake in pronouncing the word *nikoniko*, but didn't know what his sentence meant.

*　　　*　　　*

Of several expressions of the way a person laughs or smiles, *nikoniko* refers to the most pleasant, happy smile. On the other hand, *nitanita* means something quite different although it is similar in sound. *Nitanita suru* means "to grin with a malignant pleasure." Mr. Lerner was certainly lucky that Miss Yoshida was not with him when he said this.

Words directly describing manner, which are called mimesis or mimetic words, are effective when used correctly, but are liable to cause serious misunderstanding because there are so many words similar in sound and different in meaning.

When pronouncing these words, you should try to pronounce each syllable clearly, especially the second and fourth ones. Otherwise, even if you choose the right word, the listener may misunderstand. For instance, *burabura shite-imasu* (I'm loafing around) can sound like *buruburu shite-imasu* (I'm shivering with cold or fear) if the second and fourth syllables are pronounced too softly. In a similar way, *me-ga kurikuri shite-imasu* means someone, usually a young girl, "has large, lively, cute eyes"; if your pronunciation sounds like *kurakura* instead of *kurikuri*, the girl would be feeling dizzy.

To describe a person working diligently, one says

Kotsukotsu hataraite-imasu.
こつこつ　はたらいています。

But a student we once had made a mistake in saying this; his sentence sounded like

Kosokoso hataraite-imasu.

This means "He's working stealthily" implying that the person is engaged in some illegal business or something he should be ashamed of.

Oishisoo-desu-ne
おいしそうですね
(It looks good)

A few days ago Miss Yoshida brought to the office a cake she had made the previous day. The several people who gathered around the cake admired it lavishly before they ate it. Mr. Lerner also wanted to express his appreciation and said

Oishiku miemasu-ne.

meaning "It looks good." But Miss Yoshida didn't seem to be pleased and repeated *mieru?* in a somewhat displeased tone. Mr. Takada said that Mr. Lerner should have said

Oishisoo-desu-ne.
おいしそうですね。

instead. He added that Mr. Lerner's sentence could imply that the cake was not as good as it looked.

＊　　　＊　　　＊

. . . *soo* is added to various words and gives the meaning of ". . . looking." For instance, *oishii* means "delicious" while *oishisoo* means "delicious-looking"; *genkina hito* means "a healthy person" while *genkisoona hito* means "a person who looks healthy." When someone meets an acquaintance whom he has not seen for some time, he often greets him by saying

Ogenkisoo-desu-ne
or
Ogenkisoo-de, kekkoo-desu-ne.

Both mean "I'm glad to see you looking fine."

Expressions with . . . *soo* usually do not imply that the appearance is different from the reality while expressions with *mieru* usually imply a difference between the appearance and the reality. Therefore, *yosasoo-desu-ne* simply means "it looks good" or "it sounds good," but *yoku miemasu-ne* usually implies that it won't be as good as it looks. Sometimes *mieru* is added to expressions ending in . . . *soo* as in *oishisoo-ni mieru* or *yosasoo-ni mieru*; these also often imply that the appearance is different from what the thing actually is.

Another . . . *soo* is added to the dictionary form of verbs, adjectives and others to mean "I heard . . ." Thus

Furu-soo-desu.

means "I heard that it's going to rain," while

Furisoo-desu.

means "It looks like it's going to rain." The difference between "*u*" and "*i*" preceding . . . *soo* makes quite a difference in meaning.

Watashi-nanka. . .
わたしなんか……
(Someone like me. . .)

Yesterday afternoon when Mr. Lerner was talking with several colleagues, someone mentioned a TV quiz program that offered a large sum of money for the winner. Mr. Takada said that Miss Yoshida was good at answering quizzes and suggested that she try. But she laughed and said

Watashi-nanka. . .　　わたしなんか……

which literally means "Such a person as I. . ." Mr. Lerner waited for her to continue, but she didn't say anything after that, and everyone there seemed to understand and stopped discussing the subject.

＊　　　＊　　　＊

. . .nanka is a familiar equivalent of . . .nado (such as. . ., . . .and others), and helps emphasize the speaker's emotion in familiar speech. As can be seen in Miss Yoshida's sentence above, it is usually used before a negative statement. When she said Watashi-nanka . . ., she meant that she was not good at that. Saying Ano-hito-nanka kirai-desu sounds stronger than Ano-hito-wa kirai-desu (I don't like him), and sometimes Ano-hito-nanka is enough to convey the meaning without saying kirai-desu, when the listener can understand this from the context.

Because of its negative implication, it is often used with such words as doose (after all) or doomo (indeed). Doose watashi-nanka. . . (After all I'm not good enough) sounds more emphatic

90

Doose watashi-wa. . ., and *Watashi-nanka doomo. . .* (I'm not good, indeed) sounds more humble than *Watashi-wa doomo. . .*

Sometimes . . .*nanka* is used in affirmative statements too, and that is usually when the speaker is giving an example or asking someone's opinion. For instance *Ano-hito-nanka ii-desu-ne* (*lit.* A person like him is good, isn't he?) means that he is a representative of a suitable person, while saying *Ano-hito-wa ii-desu-ne* (*lit.* As for him, he is good, isn't he?) implies that the speaker is concerned only with him and with no other persons. Also, *Ano-hito-nanka doo-desu-ka* (What about him? — *lit.* How is such a person as he?) is used as a more indirect and reserved expression than *Ano-hito-wa doo-desu-ka* (*lit.* As for him, how is he?)

To a person who is wondering how he should spend his free time, someone may say

Nichiyoo-daiku-nanka doo-desu-ka.
(How about home carpentry? — *lit.* How about a Sunday carpenter?)

If the answer is

Nichiyoo-daiku-nanka. . .

it means he is not interested in it or he doesn't like it. On the other hand if the answer is

Watashi-nanka. . .

the speaker means that home carpentry is too difficult for him.

Oite-oite-kudasai
おいておいてください
(Please leave it)

Yesterday afternoon Mr. Lerner took a paper to Miss Yoshida for her to type for him. She was busy typing and could not take it in her hand, so she said

Sumimasen-ga, soko-ni oite-oite-kudasai.
すみませんが、そこに　おいておいてください。
(Sorry, please leave it there.)

Mr. Lerner understood and left the paper on her desk, but he wondered why she had said *oite-oite-kudasai* to mean "please leave it." To mean this, *oite-kudasai* should be enough because the verb *oku* from which *oite* is derived means "to leave or to place something somewhere."

*　　*　　*

When the verb *oku* is added to another verb as in *oite-oku* it means that one does something for future use. By *soko-ni oite-oite-kudasai* Miss Yoshida meant "please place it there so that I can take care of it later." The second *oite* is added to imply that the action of placing the paper on the desk will be of use in the future.

This *oku* is used most often when one does something beforehand so that things will go well. For instance, one should *denwa-o kakete-oku* (call beforehand) when visiting someone. A student works hard when he anticipates a quiz or test; this is called *benkyoo-shite-oku* (studying beforehand).

Besides being used when something is done for an immediate future as in calling someone before visiting him, *oku* is also added to verbs when the action is done for some indefinite future. For example,

hoken-o kakete-oku

means to insure one's life or property against what may happen sometime in the future — an accident, for instance.

Nowadays many young unmarried women go traveling abroad, saying

ima-no uchi-ni ryokoo-shite-oku.

which literally means "I will go traveling now for the future." The implication is that they won't be able to go traveling as freely after they get married and have a family.

Onna-no-hito
女の人
(A woman)

A few days ago when Mr. Lerner was leaving his office, he met a woman in the hall who wanted to see Mr. Takada. So he went back to where Mr. Takada was and told him

Takada-san, onna-ga ai-ni kimashita.

meaning "A woman is here to see you, Mr. Takada." Mr. Takada looked surprised and the several people working in the room laughed a lot. After a while Miss Yoshida said

'Onna-no-hito' *-deshoo?*
「女の人」でしょう？

Mr. Lerner said yes, and the people stopped laughing.

What was wrong with calling a woman *onna* instead of *onna-no-hito*? What difference is there between the two?

*　　*　　*

It is true that *onna* means a woman and *otoko* a man, but these two words are rather limited in their usage.

One usage is to emphasize a person's sex rather than his or her being a human being as in:

Kono shigoto-wa onna-niwa mukanai. (This work is not suited to women.)
Otoko-wa sebiro-o kiru. (Men wear suits.)

In these sentences, *otoko* and *onna* are not used

to refer to a specific person. Referring to someone as *otoko* or *onna* sounds very familiar and must be avoided in polite speech. Instead, usually *otoko-no-hito* is used to mean "a man" and *onna-no-hito* to mean "a woman."

Otoko-no stands for "male" and *onna-no* stands for "female": thus, *onna-no-hito* literally means a female person. In the same way *onna-no-ko* (*lit.* female child) means "girl" and *otoko-no-ko* "boy." A male teacher is called *otoko-no sensee* and a woman doctor is *onna-no oishasan*.

Another usage of *otoko* and *onna* is in referring to a specific person, but this is limited to very familiar conversation. Only between good friends or in familiar speech does one say

Ii otoko-da. (He is a nice guy.) instead of
Ii hito-desu. (He is a nice man.)

Sometimes *otoko* and *onna* mean someone's lover, usually illegitimate or secret, in vulgar speech. Therefore Mr. Lerner's sentence *onna-ga ai-ni kimashita* sounded as if Mr. Takada were a gangster hiding himself from the police and his mistress had come to see him. Mr. Lerner should have said

Okyakusan-desu. (Someone had come to see you.)
   or
Dareka onna-no-hito-ga kite-imasu. (There's a woman to see you.)

Moo ichido itte-kudasai
もう いちど いってください
(Please say it once more)

Last Sunday afternoon when Mr. Lerner was reading at home, his landlord Mr. Takahashi came to see him. After a short business discussion, the two men talked about various things. When Mr. Takahashi referred to his plans for the weekend, Mr. Lerner couldn't understand him very well, so he asked him to repeat it, saying

Moo ichido itte-kudasai.
もう いちど いってください。
(Please say it once more.)

Then immediately he thought this might have sounded too abrupt, so he corrected himself by saying *Moo ichido osshatte-kudasai.* But Mr. Takahashi had an unpleasant look for a moment before he repeated his statement.

*　　　*　　　*

Moo ichido itte-kudasai or *Moo ichido!* is a kind of classroom Japanese; a teacher may tell his students to repeat by saying this, but it cannot be used in more social situations. Changing *itte* into *osshatte* (a more polite verb meaning "say") does not produce any remarkable change.

An English-speaking person may wonder what the Japanese equivalent of "I beg your pardon?" or "Would you mind saying that again?" is, but it is not simple to decide on the Japanese equivalent.

In English, one can politely ask someone to repeat what he has said, but in Japanese, one should hesitate to ask someone to repeat what he has said when one has to be polite, because it might embarrass the other. Therefore instead of directly making a request, one should try to accomplish his request by other means.

In normal communication between Japanese, the listener usually gives *aizuchi* (reply word) like *Ee*, *Hai*, or *Un* to show that he has understood so far and the speaker can go on. If the listener doesn't give *aizuchi* when expected, or says *Ha?* or *E?* in a rising tone, the speaker senses that the listener hasn't understood well, and repeats on his own accord. In this case, no verbal request to repeat is made.

Or, sometimes one says something like

Chotto yoku wakarimasen-deshita-ga . . .
(I didn't quite understand . . .)

This explains what situation the listener is in and leaves the solution to the speaker, who will repeat without being verbally asked to do so.

Hitoyama kudasai
ひとやま　ください
(Please give me one heap)

Last Friday evening Mr. Lerner dropped in at a fruit shop on his way home. He wanted some apples. There were several flat baskets with five or six apples piled up. He said to the woman in the store

Ringo-o **hitotsu** *kudasai.*
りんごを　**ひとつ**　ください。

meaning "Please give me one (basket of) apples." But the woman looked embarrassed and said that she couldn't sell one apple alone. So he pointed to the basket and told her *Kore-o hitotsu kudasai* (*lit.* Please give one of this). Then she said

Aa, **hitoyama** *-desu-ka.*
ああ、**ひとやま**ですか。

and gave him the apples gladly.

Mr. Lerner felt that counting things in Japanese is quite difficult. He had learned several counters already but he seemed to have some more to learn.

*　　　*　　　*

Most objects are counted as *hitotsu, futatsu, mittsu* (one, two, three) etc., but there are several counters used depending on the shape of things. Thin objects like paper are counted with *-mai*, and thin, long objects like pencils are counted as *ippon, nihon, sanbon,* etc. One student who is tall and slender once wondered if people like him should be counted with *ippon*. No, human beings are counted with *hitori*, *futari*, *sannin*, etc., regardless of how big or small they are. On the other hand, small animals are counted with *-hiki* while big ones are counted with *-too*.

In addition to these counters, there are some used for collections of things. When things are piled up, *-yama* is used, as in *hitoyama*, *futayama;* when the container is a plate, things piled up on it are counted as *hitosara* (one plate); things contained in boxes are counted with *-hako*.

Counters are now in the process of being simplified; traditional counters are now often replaced by more simple counters like *hitotsu*, *futatsu*, etc., or *ikko*, *niko* (one piece, two pieces). For example, two different counters have been used for two classical Japanese instruments, the *koto* and *shamisen*, but nowadays many young people use *hitotsu* or *ikko* for either of them.

It is good to be able to use some basic counters such as *-mai*, *-hon*, *-satsu* (used for counting books), *hitori*, *-dai* (for vehicles and machines), *-ken* (for houses). It is also recommended that you know that words signifying number are usually used like adverbs. Namely, to say that you want one heap of apples, rather than saying

Hitoyama-no ringo-o kudasai.

it is more conversational to say

Ringo-o hitoyama kudasai.
りんごを　ひとやま　ください。

Kuru-to iimashita
くると いいました
(He said that he would come)

Yesterday morning Mr. Okada called and told Mr. Lerner that he was coming to see Mr. Takada and him that afternoon. So he told Mr. Takada about it, saying

Okada-san-ga kimasu-to iimashita.
(Mr. Okada said ''I will come.'')

Mr. Takada thanked him and asked if the discussions would be over by five. He answered

Owarimasu-to omoimasu.

meaning ''I think they will be finished.''

Miss Yoshida, who happened to be with them, said that Mr. Lerner's speech was overly polite. Mr. Takada didn't think it was polite; he said it sounded strange somehow. The two said they would rather say

Okada-san-ga kuru-to iimashita.
岡田さんが くると いいました。
and
Owaru-to omoimasu.
おわると おもいます。
　　　　*　　　　　*　　　　　*

In polite speech sentences usually end with *-masu*, *-mashita*, *-desu*, or other polite forms, but in quoted parts, plain forms are used as in *Kuru-to iimashita* instead of *Kimasu-to iimashita*. *Kimasu-to iimashita* is grammatically correct and can be understood, but gives the impression of inadequate skill.

For example, instead of saying *Ii-desu-to omoimasu* (I think it is good), it sounds better to say *Ii-to omoimasu*. *Ii-hito-desu-to omoimasu* (I think he's a good person) should be changed to *Ii-hito-da-to omoimasu*. This is also true when the quoted parts are in the negative; *Konai-to omoimasu* (I don't think he will come) sounds better than *Kimasen-to omoimasu*.

Or, when reporting that you were asked or told to do something, rather than saying

Kite-kudasai-to iwaremashita.
(I was told "Please come."),

it sounds better to say
Kite-kure-to iwaremashita.
(I was asked to come.)
    or
Kuru-yoo-ni iwaremashita.
(I was told to come.)

Therefore in reporting someone else's statements or telling what you think, it is recommended that you use plain forms instead of polite ones. It takes some practice, but when you do it, your Japanese will sound much more natural.

Mr. *Ukkari*
ミスターうっかり
(Mr. Inadvertent)

During the past six months or so, Mr. Lerner has given several nicknames to his colleagues from their speech habits. He showed the list to Mr. Takada and explained how he had named them. Mr. Takada praised a few of them as clever, and said that they indicated Mr. Lerner's progress in Japanese.

*   *   *

Mr. *Ukkari* うっかり

Mr. Lerner named Mr. Kato "Mr. *Ukkari*." Mr. Kato often makes mistakes when preparing papers or giving information. When his mistakes are pointed out to him, he always says

> *Ukkari machigaemashita.*
> (I inadvertently made a mistake.)

To Mr. Lerner a mistake is a mistake whether it is made inadvertently or intentionally. But somehow the Japanese are tolerant of mistakes that are made inadvertently, and Mr. *Ukkari* seems to be spared some criticism or reprimands.

Mr. *Jitsu-wa* じつは

Mr. Lerner was told that the Japanese like to say a few things before starting a discussion, and that *Jitsu-wa* is used when the speaker really starts discussing something seriously. But Mr. Sato starts any statement with *Jitsu-wa* even when it does not have to be preceded by this phrase. Mr. Lerner guesses that this habit developed from his desire to attract other people's attention. Once Mr. Lerner purposely used this phrase incorrectly in order to criticize Mr. Sato's habit. He said *Jitsu-wa kyoo-wa getsuyoobi-desu-ne* (*lit.* As a matter of fact, today is Monday). Everybody laughed but Mr. Sato himself did not seem to pay any attention. To him *Jitsu-wa* seems to have lost its original meaning.

Mr. *Muzukashii* むずかしい

Mr. Yamamoto is named "Mr. *Muzukashii*." He is a cautious man, and seldom says yes to others. Even about a very simple matter, he first says *Sore-wa muzukashii-desu-ne* (That is difficult). Mr. Lerner is thinking of asking him if one and one make two and seeing if he will say it's *muzukashii*.

And last but not least — Mr. *Issho* (Mr. Together)

Mr. Ota always asks others to do something together, saying *Issho-ni doo?* (How about doing it with me?) He never drinks coffee alone, never goes out for lunch alone, and he even asks someone else to go buy cooking stoves with him. He seems to be unable to do anything alone. This must be a reflection of the Japanese idea that it is very important to identify oneself with the members of the group. But Mr. Lerner doesn't seem to be able to get used to this. He sometimes wonders if Mr. Ota will say *Issho-ni doo?* when he is going to die.

Zannen-desu-ne
ざんねんですね
(That's too bad)

Mr. Lerner often finds it difficult to give an appropriate comment on someone's statement. For instance, when he heard that Mr. Okada's daughter had found a job, he wondered if he should say *Omedetoo-gozaimasu* (Congratulations!) or *Yokatta-desu-ne* (That's good, isn't it?). While he was wondering, Mr. Okada apparently thought that he had not understood, and repeated his statement, to Mr. Lerner's irritation. Later Mr. Takada said that one can say either of the two, or even both as

Omedetoo-gozaimasu. Yokatta-desu-ne.
(The first sounds more formal than the second.)

Then a few days later, he had a hard time trying to find a good expression when Mr. Okada told him that his son had had a traffic accident. He finally said

Zannen-desu-ne. ざんねんですね。

Mr. Okada politely thanked him for his sympathy, but he felt that his comment was awkward somehow.

*   *   *

Zannen-desu-ne is used when the speaker has been disappointed by something, and thinks that the person involved must be disappointed too. Therefore, when someone has failed in his exams or realizing his wishes, it is proper to say

104

this. But this expression is not used in the case of a traffic accident or the like, because that is not a matter of disappointment but of misfortune. If the accident is not very serious and only causes some trouble, one says

Taihen-desu-ne. (It must be tough.)

If the accident has caused injury or sickness, one says

Sore-wa ikemasen-ne. Odaiji-ni.
(That's too bad. Take good care of yourself.)

This expression can be used when someone has caught a cold or been taken ill.

But when the accident has caused death, or in other cases of bereavement, one usually expresses his surprise and sorrow by other means. As verbal expressions, there are such phrases as *Goshuushoosama-desu* (Deepest condolences) or *Kono tabi-wa tonda koto-de* . . . (This time it is really terrible). But usually one just says *Soo-desu-ka* . . . (Is that so?) or *Hontoo-desu-ka* (Is that true?) in an almost whispering voice. In such cases, nonverbal expressions such as dropping one's shoulders or looking down are more important. Fluent comments, especially accompanied by inappropriate nonverbal expressions, are rather damaging.

Ee, honjitsu-wa. . .
ええ、本日は……
(Well, this day is. . .)

Mr. Lerner attended the wedding of his colleague Mr. Fukuda last Sunday. Mr. Takada sat next to him and explained various things about the ceremony. During the dinner after the ceremony, several people were asked to say a few words to congratulate the newly-wed couple. Mr. Lerner noticed that every one of the speakers started his speech with *Ee. . .* and most of them said

Ee, honjitsu-wa. . .
ええ、本日は……
(Well, this day is. . .)

The rest was a series of formal expressions which were unfamiliar to Mr. Lerner. He also noticed that this *Ee. . .* is pronounced with a sustained tone while *Ee* meaning "yes" is pronounced with a falling tone.

Later he asked Mr. Takada what this *Ee. . .* meant; he said that it doesn't mean anything and is similar to *Anoo. . .* (Excuse me. . .) and *Eeto . . .* (Well).

*　　　*　　　*

It is true that *Ee. . .* is similar to *Anoo. . .* and *Eeto. . .* in that it is used when starting a statement as well as when looking for the right expression. When these words are used before starting a statement, they are a signal that the speaker is going to start talking. *Ee. . .* is used to start a formal speech made in public. It is used on occasions from ceremonious ones to the announcements of the arrival of trains at a station. *Anoo.* . . at the beginning of a speech also sounds polite but is used in personal conversation rather than in public. *Eeto.* . . sounds familiar. This *Ee.* . . is used very often because the Japanese feel that starting a public announcement without any signal is abrupt and ineffective.

Some people feel that *Ee.* . . is masculine while *Anoo.* . . is feminine. But the difference is the occasion where they are used rather than the speaker's sex. Since women so far have not been given many chances to speak in public, they haven't had many chances to use it; therefore *Ee.* . . seems unbecoming for women. This is also true of another similar expression. Some men make a hissing sound by a sharp intake of breath when starting a statement. Whether women will come to use these expressions more in the future along with changes in society is yet to be seen.

Watashi-mo sorosoro gojuu-desu-kara. . .

わたしも　そろそろ　五十ですから……

(Since I'm going to be 50 very soon . . .)

The other day when Mr. Lerner was chatting with Mr. Okada after their business discussion, Mr. Okada told him that he had to think about his life after retirement. When Mr. Lerner said that he was still too young for that, he said

Iie, watashi-mo sorosoro gojuu-desu-kara. . .
いいえ、わたしも　そろそろ　五十ですから……
(*lit.* No, since I'm also going to be 50 very soon . . .)

Mr. Lerner thought that someone else was going to be 50 since Mr. Okada had used the particle *mo* which means "too" or "also," so he later asked Mr. Takada about it. Mr. Takada said no and said that *mo* does not always mean "too"; in Mr. Okada's sentence it just meant *wa* (as for).

Then what's the difference between saying *Watashi-mo gojuu-desu* and *Watashi-wa gojuu-desu*? After this Mr. Lerner noticed that the Japanese often use *mo* when *wa* seems to be more appropriate to him.

＊　　　＊　　　＊

The particle *mo* is used in several senses; it means "also," "as much as," "about" and "even." Most often it means "also" and Mr. Okada used it in this sense.

When *mo* is used in the sense of "also," there are two cases; one is when there is some specific counterpart and the other is when there is no specific one. For example, when one says

Yoshida-san-wa   shitte-imasu.   Watashi-mo shitte-imasu.
(Miss Yoshida knows it, and I know it, too.)

there is a specific counterpart. Mr. Okada's sentence belongs to the latter usage. When he said *Watashi-mo . . .*, he wasn't thinking of anyone in particular. He meant that there are many others who are going to be 50; and that he is going to be 50 as well as those others.

This *mo* implies that the speaker is not referring to his case as being unique; he implies that he is just one of many such people. If he says *Watashi-wa* instead, he is referring only to himself.

Expressions using *mo* in this way sound philosophical as seen in such sentences as:

Otoko-mo   yonjuu   sugiru-to   tsukareyasuku naru. (Men over 40 get tired easily.)
   or
Sake-mo   sukoshi-nara   kusuri-da. (Small amounts of alcoholic beverages are good for the health.)

The Japanese sometimes go so far as to say

Ningen-mo binboo-suru-to ki-ga yowaku naru. (People become weak-willed when they're hard up for money.)

It would be strange to translate *Ningen-mo* as "Human beings as well as other beings," but the underlying idea is that human beings are also a part of nature or the universe.

Chotto sono hen-made kimashita-node. . .

ちょっと その へんまで きましたので…

(Since I happened to be in the neighborhood)

Last Sunday afternoon when Mr. Lerner was having a late lunch, someone rang the doorbell. Mr. Takahashi stood at the door. He said

Chotto sono hen-made kimashita-node. . .
ちょっと その へんまで きましたので……

(Since I happened to be in the neighbor-hood. . .)

and handed him a large gift of fruit.

Mr. Lerner asked him to come in and talked with him for about an hour. Mr. Takahashi was a pleasant person to talk with, but Mr. Lerner didn't like to have to stop eating. Why didn't Mr. Takahashi call before he showed up so that Mr. Lerner could have finished his meal? It was not like Mr. Takahashi who was always very polite and reserved.

＊　　　＊　　　＊

Just because he was polite, Mr. Takahashi visited Mr. Lerner without previous announcement. (Most probably he didn't happen to be in the neighborhood; he came to visit Mr. Lerner.) Many Japanese feel that it is inconsiderate to tell someone that they want to visit because if the visitor has announced his arrival the host must work hard to make preparations for him. It is more considerate to visit someone just casually without giving any previous notice. And in such a visit, this expression *Chotto sono hen-made*

110

kimashita-node. . . is used.

Sono hen literally means "the neighborhood I have referred to"; the speaker uses the word *sono* because he wants to give an impression as if he has already specified the place, although he actually hasn't. Sometimes its synonym *soko* is used in place of *sono hen*. Both *Chotto soko-made* and *Chotto sono hen-made* are used to mean "Just down the street" in reply to the set expression *Dochira-e?* (*lit.* Where are you going?).

The expression *Chotto sono hen-made kima-shita-node* implies that the visit is casual and so the host doesn't have to worry about his unclean rooms or poor refreshment. It also implies that the visitor expects to be excused from bringing a bigger gift for the host.

This is closely related to the idea that one has to make great efforts to entertain a guest. The guest has to be received into a perfectly clean room, be given the best food the family can afford, and see the host and his family properly dressed.

Many Japanese find it difficult to decide which way to choose — either to visit someone without appointment in this traditional way or to make an appointment in order not to interrupt the host's schedule.

Arigatoo-gozaimashita
ありがとうございました
(Thank you for having been so kind)

A few weeks ago Mr. Lerner was asked to give a short speech at a gathering of several dozen businessmen, and talked about his experiences in Japan. When his speech came to an end, he said with a bow

Doomo arigatoo-gozaimasu.
(Thank you very much.)

to thank the audience for listening to his inadequate Japanese.

The audience remained silent for a moment as if they expected him to say something else before they clapped their hands in applause.

Later, Mr. Takada said that Mr. Lerner should have said

Arigatoo-gozaimashita.
ありがとうございました。

instead of *Arigatoo-gozaimasu.* After that Mr. Lerner noticed that the Japanese sometimes use this expression *Arigatoo-gozaimashita* in place of *Arigatoo-gozaimasu*, but he didn't understand the difference between the two.

*   *   *

When giving factual information, whether one should use the present tense or the past is decided by the facts themselves; you have to say *Kinoo ame-ga furimashita* to mean "It rained yesterday and *Kotoshi sanjuu-desu* to mean "I am now 30 years old." But when expressing feelings,

112

one chooses the tense depending on how one feels. To thank someone, one can use either the present or the past. If one feels that he is grateful now for the favor that someone has done him, he says *Arigatoo-gozaimasu*. If he feels that he should emphasize that the favor has been completed after the passage of some time, he says *Arigatoo-gozaimashita* to mean "Thank you for having been so kind."

The form ending in *-ta* as in *furimashita* or *gozaimashita* is different in its usage from the English verbs in their past forms. Japanese verbs ending in *-ta* (or, sometimes in *-da*) are used to indicate that an action has been completed regardless of whether it took place in the past, takes place in the present, or even in the future. One says *Ashita okita toki-ni denwa-shimasu* (*lit*. I will call you when I have woken up tomorrow).

Because *Arigatoo-gozaimashita* signifies that the favor has been completed after the lapse of some time it is appropriate for the speaker to use it when he has completed his speech. Similarly, when one leaves someone after a long time, he often says

Nagai aida arigatoo-gozaimashita.
(*lit*. Thank you for having been kind to me for a long time.)

De, kyoo-wa. . . ?

で、きょうは……

(Well, what can I do for you today?)

The other day Mr. Matsumoto came to see Mr. Lerner and Mr. Takada. He obviously came to discuss some business, but he didn't start talking about it immediately; he talked about his favorite baseball player. Mr. Lerner knew that it is customary for many Japanese businessmen to spend some time like this before a discussion, so he waited patiently for him to start discussing business saying *Jitsu-wa. . .* (As a matter of fact). But Mr. Takada didn't wait long. He agreed with Mr. Matsumoto about the player being the best, and before Mr. Matsumoto started to say anything else, he said

De, kyoo-wa. . .?
で、きょうは……？
(*lit.* Then, today. . .?)

with a sustained tone. Then Mr. Matsumoto immediately started discussing business, and the talk was finished in an amazingly short time.

Mr. Lerner was surprised that Japanese businessmen are not always willing to spend a lot of time in preliminary talk, and that they can make it very short if they want to.

*   *   *

It is customary and regarded as good in Japan to spend some time talking leisurely so that good relations between the two people can be established before the business is discussed. But at the same time, it is also true that sometimes people start discussing business very soon after they meet. In such cases people usually say

De, kyoo-wa. . .?
or
Kyoo-wa nanika. . .? (*lit.* As for today, any-thing. . .?)

to mean "What can I do for you?"

These expressions can be taken as abbrevia-tions of longer sentences. After *De, kyoo-wa. . .?*, *nan-no goyoo-desu-ka* (*lit.* what business do you have?) or *nanika goyoo-desu-ka* (*lit.* do you have some business?) is left out. After *Kyoo-wa na-nika. . .?* various things can be meant without being mentioned. They can be *arimashita-ka* (did anything happen?), *tokubetsu-no ohanashi-ga ari-masu-ka* (is there something in particular you want to talk about?) or *okomari-no koto-demo arimasu-ka* (do you have anything that troubles you?).

What is important is that these sentences are not completed in polite inquiries. Saying them out loud sounds rather coarse and impolite; *nanika* is enough and nothing more should be said out loud when one has to be polite. Sometimes just *ari-masu-ka* is left out as in *Kyoo-wa nanika toku-betsu-no ohanashi-demo. . .?* In this type of ex-pression, *-demo* is preferred to *-ga*.

Taihen kekkoo-da-to omoimasu
たいへん けっこうだと おもいます
(I think it's very good)

Yesterday afternoon the director of the company, Mr. Mori, asked Mr. Lerner and Mr. Takada to come to his office, and explained his plan for developing a new system to improve the company's business. When he finished his explanation and asked the two men to comment on it, Mr. Takada said

Taihen kekkoo-da-to omoimasu.
たいへん けっこうだと おもいます。
(I think it's very good.)

So Mr. Lerner thought that there would be no further discussion between Mr. Mori and Mr. Takada, and that it was his turn to state his opinion. When he was about to do so, Mr. Mori asked Mr. Takada again if there was any respect in which it could be improved. Then Mr. Takada said

Soo-desu-nee. . . (Well . . .)

and paused. Mr. Mori prompted him to continue. Mr. Takada said

Machigatte-iru-kamo shiremasen-ga . . .
(I may be wrong but . . .)

Mr. Mori told him that he should stop worrying and go ahead.

Finally Mr. Takada pointed out one place that he thought might be changed. Mr. Lerner thought that now Mr. Takada was finished and it was his turn, but it wasn't. Mr. Mori again wondered if there were any other points that Mr. Takada thought should be revised!

*   *   *

It is not easy to criticize someone else without hurting his feelings in any society, but it takes more time and consideration in polite conversation in Japanese. When someone has made a proposal and invites criticism, one usually first expresses one's appreciation; Mr. Takada first said that he thought the plan to be very good. And when one is urged to state his opinion, he does not immediately start stating it but shows his hesitation, as Mr. Takada did in saying *Soodesu-nee*. Mr. Mori again prompted him but he indicated his apprehension that he might be wrong in order to ascertain that Mr. Mori was fully ready for his criticism.

Our students often ask what expressions should be used to state their criticism politely in Japanese, but mere repetition of verbal expressions will not work. It is much more important to try to find the right moment when one can express himself without damaging his good relations with the listener.

Chotto otera-e itte-kimasu
ちょっと お寺へ いってきます
(I'm going to the temple)

Mr. Lerner has come to be able to express himself in Japanese more freely than before, but he still has some trouble with pronunciation. A few days ago Mr. Okada came to discuss some business with Mr. Lerner and Mr. Takada. After the discussion and some leisurely talk, Mr. Okada looked at his watch and said *Dewa, kore-de* (*lit.* Now with this) to take his leave. Mr. Lerner thought that he might as well say something nice to retain him instead of immediately saying good-bye, so he said

Moo kaerimasu-ka.
(Are you leaving so soon?)

But Mr. Okada looked puzzled for a moment, and then said that business is rather difficult at present and his company wasn't making much money. This time Mr. Lerner felt puzzled.

Mr. Takada realized what was wrong and said that Mr. Lerner had said

Mookarimasu-ka.
(Are you making a lot of money?)

when trying to say *Moo kaerimasu-ka.*

Then, just yesterday when Mr. Lerner was taking a walk in the park with Miss Winters and Miss Yoshida, Miss Winters stopped and asked them to wait a minute, saying

Chotto **otearai-e** *itte-kimasu-kara.*

118

ちょっと　お手洗いへ　いってきますから。
(I'm going to the rest room.)

Mr. Lerner said OK but Miss Yoshida asked *Doo-shite?* (Why?) The other two were surprised. After a funny exchange the three people found out that what Miss Winters had said sounded like

Chotto **otera-e** *itte-kimasu-kara.*
ちょっと　お寺へ　いってきますから。
(I'm going to the temple.)

＊　　　　＊　　　　＊

When pronouncing Japanese words it is important to say each sound unit with approximately the same length. English speakers have to be particularly careful when pronouncing words that include successive vowels like *otearai* or *kaeru*. They tend to say two vowels together instead of as two different sound units; thus their *otearai* tends to sound like *otera* and *kaeru* like *karu*. Therefore Mr. Lerner's *moo kaerimasu-ka* sounded like *mookarimasu-ka*.

To the Japanese ear the word *otearai* consists of five sound units. If you pronounce the successive two vowels *ea* and *ai* together, your *otearai* will sound like a word consisting of three units instead of five. Lack of attention toward the number of sound units in a word leads to misunderstanding; *obasan* (aunt or woman) and *obaa-san* (grandmother or old woman) must be distinguished, and if you say *oobasan* it means "Mr. Ooba" or "Ms. Ooba."

Rainen-ga yoi toshi-de arimasu yoo-ni

来年が　よい　年で　あります　ように
(May next year be a good one)

Mr. Lerner has noticed that the Japanese seem to be highly conscious of the year changing between December and January. Even early in December people often say that the remainder of this year is rapidly decreasing. Just yesterday Mr. Lerner heard a master of ceremonies for a TV program, after looking back on what had happened during the year, say

Rainen-ga yoi toshi-de arimasu yoo-ni.
来年が　よい　年で　あります　ように。
(May next year be a good one.)

Here again the sentence is not completed. Mr. Lerner sensed that something is left unmentioned after this phrase, but he didn't know what that might be.

*　　　*　　　*

. . .*yoo-ni* by itself means "in the way. . ." or "so that. . ." For example, *Ma-ni au yoo-ni hayaku demashita* means "I left early so that I could be on time." And *kaze-o hikanai yoo-ni ki-o tsukete-imasu* means "I take care so that I won't catch a cold." People use . . .*yoo-ni shite-kudasai* (please behave so as to. . .) when asking others to do something which requires some effort. *Kaze-o hikanai yoo-ni shite-kudasai* means "please take care not to catch a cold" and *ashi-ta-wa hayaku kuru yoo-ni shite-kudasai* means "please try to come early tomorrow."

After *rainen-ga yoi toshi-de arimasu yoo-ni*

(so that next year will be a good one) such phrases as *oinori-shimasu* (I pray for you) or *ino-rimashoo* (let's pray) are understood and left out.

There are several formal expressions ending in . . .*yoo-ni* which are used to wish others good luck.

Ichinichi-mo hayaku ogenki-ni nararemasu yoo-ni.

(I hope you will be better very soon — *lit.* So that you will become healthy even one day earlier.)

is said to someone who is sick or to someone whose family member is sick.

These expressions are formal; they are used either in very polite conversations or in letters. Well, presuming that this year has been a good one for you, let us say

Rainen-MO yoi toshi-de arimasu yoo-ni.
(May next year ALSO be a good one.)

Chotto muri-desu-wa
ちょっと むりですわ
(It's rather difficult)

The other day Mr. Lerner and Mr. Takada were leaving the office to go on a series of business visits to several companies. Miss Yoshida asked them if they could come back to the office before five. Mr. Lerner answered

Chotto muri-desu-wa.
ちょっと むりですわ。

meaning "that's rather difficult" (*lit.* it is a little unreasonable). Then Miss Yoshida burst out laughing and said she didn't like to be teased. Mr. Lerner didn't understand what was wrong with his Japanese.

Mr. Takada explained that a sentence ending with *wa* sounds purely feminine and Miss Yoshida suspected that he was imitating her. No, Mr. Lerner said. He just added *wa* because he had heard Mr. Nishikawa say several sentences with *wa*. Mr. Takada and Miss Yoshida admitted that Mr. Nishikawa had used *wa* many times, but they still thought Mr. Lerner's use of *wa* sounded funny.

*   *   *

The particle *wa* is used at the end of sentences to indicate emphasis by both men and women, but the pitch is quite different between men and women. When used by men it is added with a low pitch as in

Chotto muri-desu

-wa.

while women usually add *wa* with a high pitch as

in

-wa.

Chotto muri-desu

Another difference is that the use of *wa* by men is rather limited; generally speaking, middle-aged men use it much more often than young men, and it is usually added to the polite forms ending in *-desu* or *-masu*. On the other hand women of all ages use it and it can be added either to the polite or the plain form.

Women sometimes use *no* at the end of sentences as in

Moo owarimashita-no.
(It's over now.)

This *no* is used to explain when said with a falling tone. When used with a rising tone it signifies a question. Men use it only with questions.

Among the several sentence particles, *ne* and *yo* are used most often; they are used regardless of age, sex and level. But other particles such as *wa, no, na, sa, zo,* and *ze* are rather limited in their usage, and in using them one has to be very careful to choose the right one and the right tone.

Sore-ni shite-mo
それに　しても
(Even so)

A few days ago several people including Mr. Lerner were waiting for Mr. Okada to come to the office to discuss some business. Since he didn't show up on time, they started talking. Someone mentioned that he had not been skiing for a few years and they discussed skiing for a while. When that discussion came to an end Mr. Takada looked at his watch and said

> *Sore-ni shite-mo Okada-san osoi-desu-ne.*
> それに　しても　岡田さん　おそいですね。
> (Even so, Mr. Okada is late, isn't he?)

Everybody agreed and someone was starting to call him, when Mr. Okada showed up with an apology that the traffic had been very bad.

Mr. Lerner didn't understand the meaning of the phrase *sore-ni shite-mo*, so he later consulted a dictionary. He found several English equivalents such as "even so," "for all that," "still," "nevertheless," "although," and "admitting that." But none of them seemed to fit the sentence Mr. Takada had used. What relation did the discussion of skiing have with Mr. Okada's being late?

*　　　*　　　*

Sore-ni shite-mo literally means "even though we decide on that"; it is used when expressing one's opinion about something else after admitting what has already been said either by oneself or by another speaker. For instance, suppose two people are wondering why someone is late.

A: *Michi-ga konde-iru-n-deshoo.* (I guess he is late because the traffic is heavy.)

B: *Sore-ni shite-mo konna-ni okureru hazu-wa nai-deshoo.* (But he shouldn't be as late as this.)

Here *sore-ni shite-mo* means "admitting what you have said," or "although he may be delayed by the heavy traffic."

This example is easy to understand because we can clearly see what *sore* refers to, but in Mr. Takada's sentence above, *sore-ni shite-mo* seems difficult to understand because *sore* does not refer to what has been said immediately before. Here, *sore* is used to refer, not to the ski topic which directly precedes it, but to the fact that the people there have been waiting for Mr. Okada. Thus *sore-ni shite-mo* can be paraphrased as "although we have been waiting for him, killing time by discussing things like skiing." *Sore* is usually used to refer to what the speaker or someone else has said, but sometimes it can refer to what has been the topic or the concern of the people engaged in the conversation.

Shinde-imasu
死んでいます
(I'm dead)

Since the beginning of the new year Mr. Lerner has been very busy. When Miss Yoshida asked him yesterday if he was still busy, he answered that he was, and added, by way of exaggeration,

Shinde-imasu.
死んでいます。

to mean "I'm dying." Miss Yoshida looked puzzled. So he changed the verb and said

Taorete-imasu.

to mean "I'm about to collapse." But Miss Yoshida didn't understand. She even asked him *Nani-ga* (What is?).

Later he found out that he should have said

Shinisoo-desu.
死にそうです。
　　　or
Taoresoo-desu.

He also found that *shinde-imasu* means someone is dead and *taorete-imasu* means somebody or something has fallen.

＊　　　　＊　　　　＊

The *te-imasu* form as in *shinde-imasu* is often used in a different way from the English ". . .ing" form. The *te-imasu* form in its main usage is used to indicate either an action in progress as in *hon-o yonde-imasu* (I'm now reading a book) or a state of being resulting from the completion of an action as in *kekkon-shite-imasu* (I'm married) or *yasete-imasu* (I'm thin — *lit.* I have grown thin).

"I'm dying" or "I'm leaving very soon" indicate an action which is going to take place in the near future, but *shinde-imasu* or *dekakete-imasu* cannot be used in the same way; *shinde-imasu* means that someone has died and is now dead, and *dekakete-imasu* means that someone has gone out. To mean "I'm going to die," you have to use some other expression such as *shinisoo-desu* (*lit.* it seems as if I'm going to die) or *moo sugu shinimasu* (I'm going to die soon).

We sometimes hear English speakers use the *te-imasu* form to indicate future action or future plans as in *kuji-ni basu-ni notte-imasu* (I'll be riding in a bus at nine) or *ashita-mo koko-de hataraite-imasu* (I'll be working here tomorrow, too). These sentences sound strange to the Japanese ear. You should say *kuji-ni basu-ni norimasu* or *ashita-mo koko-de hataraku tsumori-desu* (*lit.* I plan to work here tomorrow, too).

Yoshida-san-ga kureta-n-desu
吉田さんが くれたんです
(Miss Yoshida gave it to me)

One afternoon last week, Miss Yoshida brought several tickets for a baseball game which she didn't need to the office and gave one to Mr. Lerner saying

Ichimai agemasu. (I'll give you one.)

Some time later Mr. Takada came in and asked if Mr. Lerner had bought the ticket. He answered

Iie, Yoshida-san-ga ageta-n-desu.
(*lit.* No, it is that Miss Yoshida gave.)

meaning "No, this was given to me by Miss Yoshida." Then Mr. Takada asked to whom Miss Yoshida had given it. To whom? Mr. Lerner had learned that the Japanese do not mention *watashi* (I or me) or *watashi-ni* (to me) when it can be understood without mentioning it. While Mr. Lerner was wondering about this, Mr. Takada seemed to understand what Mr. Lerner meant to say, and told him that he should have said

Yoshida-san-ga kureta-n-desu.
吉田さんが くれたんです。
(Miss Yoshida gave it to me.)

Why couldn't the verb *ageru* be used when Mr. Lerner talked about Miss Yoshida's giving it to him?

＊　　　＊　　　＊

Ageru refers to the action of giving something to someone else; it cannot be used to refer to someone giving something to the speaker. One says *Kore-o agemasu* (I'll give this to you) when giving something to a friend, but his friend wouldn't say *Tomodachi-ga agemashita* (My friend gave it). If he did, it would sound as if he had given it away to someone else. So he will say *Tomodachi-ga kuremashita* (My friend gave it to me).

Between friends or equals, *ageru* and *kureru* are used, but when one has to be polite, *sashiageru* is used for *ageru* and *kudasaru* for *kureru*. To be more polite, Miss Yoshida would have said

Ichimai sashiagemasu.
(Please accept one. — *lit.* I'll give one to you.)

and Mr. Lerner would have said to Mr. Takada
Yoshida-san-ga kudasatta-n-desu.
(Miss Yoshida gave it to me.)

Sometimes *yaru* is used for *ageru* between good friends or family members, mostly by men.

Yoshida-san-ga oshiete-kurema-shita

吉田さんが おしえてくれました

(Miss Yoshida kindly taught me)

When Mr. Lerner was at a party at the Takadas' last Saturday, everyone sang songs and he was asked to sing one, too. He sang a Japanese song that he had learned from Miss Yoshida a few weeks before. Everyone praised him and wondered how he had learned it. He replied

Yoshida-san-ga oshiemashita.

meaning "Miss Yoshida taught me how to sing it." Then Mr. Takada said

Aa, Yoshida-san-ga oshiete-kureta-n-desu-ka.
ああ、吉田さんが おしえてくれたんですか。
(*lit.* Oh, Miss Yoshida did the favor of teaching it to you.)

He said yes, but wondered why *kureru* had to be added. He also remembered that he had had his sentences corrected in a similar way before. For instance, when he said *Yoshida-san-ga kakimashita* to mean that Miss Yoshida had written something for him, someone corrected it to *Yoshida-san-ga kaite-kuremashita.*

*   *   *

The two expressions *Yoshida-san-ga oshiemashita* and *Yoshida-san-ga oshiete-kuremashita* refer to the same fact, but the attitude of the speaker is different. Saying *Yoshida-san-ga oshiemashita* doesn't imply that the speaker is

130

grateful to her; in fact, it can sound as if Miss Yoshida taught him just because she wanted to, regardless of whether he liked it or not. In the case mentioned above, it is appropriate to say *Yoshida-san-ga oshiete-kuremashita* because he had good reason to be grateful to her. Or, he could also say *Yoshida-san-ni oshiete-moraimashita* (*lit.* I received the favor from Miss Yoshida of teaching me); this expression also implies the speaker's gratitude.

In the same way, when one receives a visitor, one usually says

Yoku kite-kuremashita.

(I'm glad you could come. — *lit.* It is good that you did me the favor of coming.)

or more politely,

Yoku kite-kudasaimashita.

Iinikui-n-desu-ga

いいにくいんですが

(I hate to say this, but)

Last week Mr. Lerner took a proposal to the director of the company, Mr. Mori. Before he started explaining it to Mr. Mori and several other people, he thought that it might be hard to understand because of his inadequate Japanese, and said

Kore-wa taihen iinikui-n-desu-ga

meaning "This is very hard to explain, but." He expected this remark to be accepted with pleasure, but on the contrary the audience looked rather unpleasant, and some of them even looked stern.

So, Mr. Lerner added that his Japanese wouldn't be good enough; then the audience looked relieved and smiled.

Later Mr. Takada told him that he should have said

Umaku setsumee-dekinai-kamo shiremasen-ga.

うまく　説明できないかも　しれませんが

(*lit.* I may not be able to explain it very well, but)

instead.

＊　　　＊　　　＊

To mean "hard to . . ." *nikui* is added to the stem of the verb as in *wakarinikui* (hard to understand) or *yominikui* (hard to read). Therefore it is grammatically correct to say *iinikui* to mean

132

"hard to say," but *iinikui* in the above context usually means "I hate to say" or "I know I shouldn't say this." *Taihen iinikui-n-desu-ga* is usually said before asking for a big favor or venturing some criticism. Therefore the audience looked prepared for some unpleasant remark when Mr. Lerner said this. (*Iinikui* can mean something else in another context; when one says *iinikui* to refer to a word, it means that the word is difficult to pronounce.)

The antonym of *wakarinikui* is *wakariyasui*; *yomiyasui hon* means "a book easy to read." We sometimes hear English speakers say *yasashiku kowaremasu* to mean *kowareyasui* (easy to break) or *yasashiku oboemasu* for *oboeyasui* (easy to learn). These expressions are strange because *yasashiku* usually means "tenderly" or "gently" rather than "easily."

From Mr. Lerner's Diary

Feb. 12, Monday

Today Mr. Mori invited Mr. Takada and me to his house. In the living room several imported and expensive-looking bottles of whiskey were line up, with only one Japanese whiskey, probably much less expensive. When Mr. Mori asked which whiskey we would like, Mr. Takada answered, pointing to the Japanese whiskey,

Kore-ga ii-desu.
これが　いいです。
(I would like this one.)

I wanted to say that I would have the same thing, but I somehow said

Kore-de ii-desu.　これで　いいです。

Then Mr. Mori smiled and Mr. Takada laughed. To embarrass me even more, Mrs. Mori was covering her mouth with her hand and trying to stop laughing.

Mr. Takada explained that . . .*ga ii-desu* means that the speaker positively likes it while . . .*de ii-desu* means that the speaker can be satisfied with it although it's not his first choice. So I actually said "The Japanese one will do."

After we started drinking, Mr. Mori recalled this and said that I should say *Anata-ga ii* (You're the one) instead of *Anata-de ii* (You'll do) if I should ask a Japanese girl to marry me.

＊　　　＊　　　＊

Feb. 15, Thursday

I made a mistake again in Japanese comprehension. Yesterday evening Mrs. Takahashi, my landlady, brought over a beautiful *furoshiki* which she had dyed herself and asked me to send it to Margaret when I was sending her something. I admired the *furoshiki* and said I had never seen such a beautiful one. Mrs. Takahashi smiled happily and said something which sounded to me like

> *Sore irimasu.*
> それ　いります。
> (I need it.)

I was confused. I thought that she had simply brought it to show me, not to give me. So I quickly handed it back to her. Then she looked puzzled and mumbled something which sounded as if I didn't like it, and hurriedly left with the *furoshiki*.

Today when I asked about it, Miss Yoshida said that Mrs. Takahashi must have said *Osore-irimasu* which means either "I'm sorry" or "Thank you very much." Most likely she thanked me for my lavish admiration, and I didn't hear the first sound of *Osoreirimasu*. おそれいります。

Omochi-shimashoo

おもちしましよう

(Let me carry it for you)

A few days ago Mr. Mori, the director of the company, was carrying a cassette tape recorder from one room to another. Mr. Takada saw him and said

Rekoodaa, omochi-shimashoo.
レコーダー、おもちしましよう。
(Let me carry the tape recorder for you.)

Mr. Lerner remembered that he had learned that it is more polite to say *omochi-shimashoo* than to say *motte-agemashoo*, and thought that he should use this expression some time.

The next day, he saw an elderly woman on the platform waiting for the train carrying a heavy bag, and offered to help her saying

Nimotsu-o mochi-shimashoo.

meaning "I will carry your luggage for you." The woman thanked him, but she hesitated before doing so, and Mr. Lerner suspected that he hadn't said the expression correctly.

*   *   *

When offering to help, it is all right to say *motte-agemashoo*, but this expression is not very polite. To seniors or older people, it is recommended that you say *omochi-shimashoo* instead. This expression is formed by adding "*o*" and "*suru*" to the stem of verbs. Mr. Lerner was right when he tried to say *Nimotsu-o omochi-shimashoo*, but he left out the "*o*" in *omochi-*

136

shimashoo, and so his sentence sounded strange. The particle "*o*" in *nimotsu-o* can be left out in conversation, so Mr. Takada said *Rekoodaa, omochi-shimashoo*, but the "*o*" in *omochi-shima-shoo* should not be left out.

It might be helpful to practice expressions such as the following which are used very often in offering help or making a proposal.

otodoke-shimashoo (I'll bring or deliver it)
　　　　　　—from the verb *todokeru*
otsutae-shimashoo (I'll tell him)
　　　　　　—from the verb *tsutaeru*
oshirase-shimashoo (I'll let you know)
　　　　　　—from the verb *shiraseru*

It requires careful practice when two "*o*" 's are used successively as in

ooshie-shimashoo (I'll tell you)
　　　　　　—from the verb *oshieru*
ookuri-shimashoo (I'll send it to you, or I'll go with you)
　　　　　　—from the verb *okuru*

Niisan-to oneesan

にいさんと　おねえさん

(Big brother and big sister)

When Mr. Lerner was invited to the Takada's last Sunday, he was introduced to Mr. Takada's younger sister Michiko. While they were having dinner together, Michiko poured beer into her brother's glass saying

Niisan, moo sukoshi doo.
(Have a little more, brother. — *lit.* older brother.)

and when she filled her sister-in-law's glass, she said

Oneesan-mo.
(You, too, sister. — *lit.* older sister.)

Mr. Lerner noticed that Michiko always used family terms when addressing the Takada couple, while they never used *imooto* (younger sister) or *imooto-san* when addressing her, but always called her by name. (Mrs. Takada added "*san*" to her name, perhaps because she is not really her sister.)

　　　*　　　　*　　　　*

Among family members it is customary in Japan for older members to call their younger members by their first names while younger members call the older members with family terms plus "*san*," "*sama*," or "*chan*." ("*san*" is most commonly used; "*sama*" is very polite, and "*chan*" is used as an endearment.) Parents usually call their children by their first names, with

138

"*chan*" when they are young; when they grow up the father usually calls them with just the name and the mother with the name plus "*san*" or "*chan*." Sometimes older children are called *nii-san* or *neesan* by their parents. The idea is that the term is often chosen from the viewpoint of the youngest member of the family.

This custom is also applied to some extent to social groups. The senior members of a group usually call the younger ones by name — usually the family name. On the other hand, the younger members call their seniors by the terms for their position. Thus students usually call their teachers *Sensee* (Teacher). The family name of the teacher is added only when it is necessary to distinguish him from other teachers. Thus it is not customary to address a teacher by name, as in *Maeda-sensee* in the classroom when no other teacher is present.

This custom is sometimes observed even among students. There is sometimes a sharp distinction between the students of one school year and another. In such cases a student addresses another student who is his senior by one year as *Senpai* (Senior). This tendency is most remarkable in groups where there is a strong sense of membership, as in sports teams.

Sassoku-desu-ga

さっそくですが

(It's so soon but)

Yesterday afternoon Mr. Okada came to see Mr. Lerner at the office. After the two men had exchanged apologies for being rude when they met last, and had talked about the season and the weather, Mr. Okada said

Sassoku-desu-ga
さっそくですが
(*lit.* It's so soon but)

and waited for Mr. Lerner to say something. Mr. Lerner guessed that this must be another expression used before starting business discussions, so he said *Ee* (Yes), and the discussions went on smoothly.

Later he consulted a dictionary and found that *sassoku* means "immediately" or "very soon." In this case too the word must not be used in its literal sense, Mr. Lerner thought, because Mr. Okada said quite a lot before he turned to this expression.

*　　*　　*

Most Japanese feel that they have to spend some time before starting to discuss business, whether they like it or not, in order to build up good relations between the speaker and the listener. After this is done, they start their business discussions with such expressions as *jitsu-wa* (as a matter of fact), *tokoro-de* (by the way), *sate* (now), or *sore-wa soo-to* (putting that aside). *Sassoku-desu-ga* or *Sassoku-desu-kedo* is one of these expressions; it means that the speaker knows that he should spend more time before bringing up his business but he would like to be allowed to start it immediately. A more polite equivalent, *Sassoku-de osoreirimasu-ga* (I'm sorry I am going to start my business so quickly), is used in more formal situations.

The underlying idea for this expression is that one should try not to cut down on the due formalities before starting one's business. This idea is seen even more clearly in letter-writing. In the traditional etiquette for letter-writing, one has to go through a series of formal expressions — describing the season and weather, inquiring after the receiver's health, apologizing for not writing sooner. But when one does not have to be very formal, one can start his business with only the word

Zenryaku.
前略

This means that what should come first is left out. This is a very convenient expression but it is solely for letters.

Shachoo-wa orimasen
社長は　おりません
(The director isn't here)

Miss Winters called Mr. Lerner at the office yesterday afternoon. Miss Yoshida answered the phone and said

Ee, Raanaa-san irasshaimasu-yo.
(Yes, Mr. Lerner is here.)

and called him to the phone. When he had finished talking and put the phone down, the phone rang again and Miss Yoshida answered it. This time she said

Shachoo-wa ima orimasen-ga.
社長は　いま　おりませんが。
(The director is not here now.)

Mr. Lerner had learned that the verb *irasshai masu* is used for referring to someone with respect while *orimasu* is used for referring to someone in a humble manner, although both mean "to be." To Miss Yoshida, Mr. Lerner should be regarded as a colleague while the director should be her boss. Why did she use the honorific verb for Mr. Lerner and the humble verb for the director? Shouldn't it be the other way around?

*　　　*　　　*

When Miss Yoshida answered Miss Winter's call, she was speaking personally. In other words, she regarded both Mr. Lerner and Miss Winters as her personal acquaintances, so she spoke politely in referring to Mr. Lerner. But when she took the phone call from someone else,

142

probably from some other company, she was speaking as a member of the company. When a person speaks as a member of the group, he identifies himself with the other members of the group. Therefore a young woman receptionist or secretary refers to her boss in a humble way when speaking with someone who represents some other group. She will even refer to her boss or colleagues without a term of respect, as in

Raanaa-wa ima orimasen.

Because this custom is supported by the sense of identification within a group, it is not observed in a group where greater importance is placed on individuals.

Kowai
こわい
(Frightening)

Last Friday afternoon Mr. Lerner was taking a walk in the park after a late lunch. The day was warm and he was enjoying this quiet time. Then he saw several middle-aged people sitting on a bench; they had apparently come to Tokyo to do the sights. Just when he passed in front of them, one of them said in a loud voice

Aa, kowai, kowai.
(Oh, how frightening.)

and the others agreed repeating *kowai, kowai.* Mr. Lerner was shocked. He knew the meaning of the word all too well; he had once said *kowai* when trying to say *kawaii* (cute) to compliment Mr. Takada's baby and everybody laughed at him.

When he returned to the office, he told his colleagues about this and asked if he looked so frightening. They said no and wondered why the sightseers had said that. Then Mr. Kato, who knows a lot about dialects, said that the word *kowai* means "I'm tired" in several dialects; the sightseers must have been complaining among themselves instead of referring to Mr. Lerner.

*　　　*　　　*

There are many dialects in Japan and misunderstanding between speakers of different dialects often causes trouble or laughter. It is sometimes very difficult to understand other dialects, but a more serious problem is that the same words are used differently from dialect to dia-

144

lect. Depending on the dialect the word *kowai* is used with various meanings such as "hard," "tired," "painful," "unpleasant," "embarrassing," and even "clever." Another example is the word *shiasatte*; this means either two days after tomorrow or three days after tomorrow depending on the dialect.

With the long history of school education and the development of the mass media, what is called *hyoojungo* (standard Japanese) can be understood all over the country, and this makes basic communication possible. But people still tend to use their dialect when expressing their feelings because they feel that standard Japanese cannot replace the expressions they have long been using to describe delicate shades of emotion.

Konna koto-o itte-wa nan-desu-ga
こんな ことを いっては なんですが
(Probably I shouldn't say this, but)

A few days ago Mr. Lerner was chatting with Mr. Okada and several other people after a business discussion. Mr. Kato smoked a lot in the room and the air became rather bad. After Mr. Kato left the room Mr. Lerner started to open the window. Then Mr. Okada said

Konna koto-o itte-wa nan-desu-ga.
こんな ことを いっては なんですが
(*lit.* Saying such a thing is what, but.)

While Mr. Lerner was wondering what *nan-desu-ga* meant, Mr. Okada continued and said that Mr. Kato should have asked the others for permission to smoke.

The next day, before he found out the meaning of the phrase *nan-desu-ga*, Miss Yoshida came to him and asked him to correct her letter in English to her pen pal, saying

Konna koto-o onegai-shite-wa nan-desu-kedo.
(*lit.* Asking such a thing is what.)

*　　　*　　　*

The expression *nan-desu-ga* or *nan-desu-kedo* means "it's something I shouldn't do." *Konna koto-o itte-wa nan-desu-ga* means "This is something I shouldn't say, but"; this is said before venturing some criticism. Before asking a favor which seems too big or too irrelevant, one says *Konna koto-o onegai-shite-wa nan-desu-ga* meaning "This is something I shouldn't ask you, but.''

Sometimes *nan-desu-kedo* is used by itself to show one's hesitation as in

Anoo . . . nan-desu-kedo, jitsu-wa . . .
(Excuse me, . . . well, as a matter of fact . . .)

Especially in polite conversation it is regarded as good to show hesitation before giving criticism. The following expressions might be useful:

Konna koto-wa itte-wa ikenai-to omoi-masu-ga
(I know I shouldn't say such a thing, but)
Watashi-no omoichigai-kamo shiremasen-ga
(I may be wrong, but)

POLITE CONVERSATIONAL EXPRESSIONS

To communicate fully, one has to be able, not only to make grammatically correct sentences, but to carry on the conversation in the proper way. Namely, one has to know how to start talking, how to respond, and how to develop the conversation. In order to illustrate how the Japanese like to develop polite conversations, we have listed, in the following nine pages, several basic expressions together with sample conversations.

The basic expressions are divided into two categories. Expressions in the first category are used in conversations with close friends or with someone with whom you don't have to be reserved. Expressions in the second category are used when you have to be reserved and must be careful not to hurt the listener's feelings. Consequently, the latter expressions are more indirect and roundabout — not only in phrasing but also in the development of the conversation.

Because of limited space, we have listed only a few fundamental expressions. But we hope that if you read them carefully, noticing the contrasts between the two types of communication, you will easily see in what ways the Japanese try to be polite.

1. STATING ONE'S OPINION

□basic expressions:
1. *(watashi-wa)* . . . *to omoimasu* (I think . . .)
2. . . . *n-ja nai-deshoo-ka* (it might be . . .)
   . . . *n-ja nai-ka-to omoimasu* (I think it might be . . .)

□examples:
1. A: *Kono an-ni tsuite minasan doo omoimasu-ka.* (What do you think of this plan?)
   B: *Kekkoo-da-to omoimasu.* (I think it is fine.)
   C: *Watashi-mo ii-to omoimasu.* (I think it is good, too.)
   D: *Watashi-wa chotto hiyoo-ga kakarisugiru-to omoimasu.* (I think it costs too much.)
2. A: *Kono an-ni tsuite minasan-no okangae-wa doo-deshoo.* (What do you think of this plan?)
   B: *Ii-n-ja nai-deshoo-ka.* (I think it should be fine.)
   C: *Watashi-mo sore-de ii-n-ja nai-ka-to omoimasu.* (I think it should be good, too.)
   D: *Watashi-wa chotto . . .* (I think a little differently.)
   A: *Mazui-deshoo-ka.* (Do you think it won't work?)
   D: *Ee, soo-desu-ne, chotto hiyoo-ga . . .* (Well, I should think it costs . . .)
   A: *Hiyoo-desu-ka.* (You mean the cost?)
   D: *Ee, chotto kakarisugiru-n-ja nai-ka-to omoimasu-ga . . .* (Yes, it seems to me it will cost a little too much, but . . .)

Notes: For stating one's opinions . . . *to omoimasu* is the most fundamental expression; *watashi-wa* is used only when you have to distinguish yourself from others.

The conversation in example 1 illustrates a case where the participants can speak frankly and freely. The conversation in example 2 illustrates a case where the speakers are trying to be polite. In polite conversations such endings as . . . *n-ja nai-deshoo-ka* or . . . *n-ja nai-ka-to omoimasu* or . . . *no yoona ki-ga shimasu* (I have a feeling that . . .) are often used.

It is regarded as good to end the sentence with *-deshoo-ka*, . . . *ga* or . . . *kedo*, instead of ending it with *-desu* or *-masu*, so that you will sound as if you're inviting the listener to state his own opinions.

149

2. ASKING FOR OPINIONS

□**basic expressions:**

1. *doo omoimasu-ka*; *iken-o itte-kudasai*
   (what do you think?; please give your opinion)

2. *goiken* } *-o doozo*; *ikaga-desu-ka*; *doo-deshoo*
   okangae }
   (please give your opinion; what do you think?;
   I wonder what you think)

□**examples:**

1. A: *Minasan, doo omoimasu-ka.* (What do you
      think, everyone?)
   B: *Kekkoo-da-to omoimasu.* (I think it's fine.)
   A: *Kawakami-san, iken-o itte-kudasai.* (Mr.
      Kawakami, please give your opinion.)
   C: *Watashi-wa chotto chigaimasu.* (I think a
      little differently.)

2. A: *Minasan-no okangae-o doozo.* (Please give
      your opinion.)
   BCD: . . . . .
   A: *Doozo goenryo naku.* (Please feel free to
      give your opinions.)
   BCD: . . . . .
   A: *Kawakami-san, doo-deshoo.* (What do you
      think, Mr. Kawakami?)
   C: *Soo-desu-nee.* (Well. . .)
   A: *Donna koto-demo kekkoo-desu-kara.* . .
      (Anything is all right, so. . .)
   C: *Ja, hitotsu watashi-no kangae-o iwasete-ita-
      dakimasu-ga.* . . (Well, then, let me say a
      few words.)

Notes: In polite conversations the Japanese do not immediately give their opinions. It is rather common, as in example
2, that the chairman has to ask several times before anyone
starts talking. This comes sometimes from the feeling that
one should be modest and inconspicuous, and sometimes from
the feeling that the senior members of the group should first
be given a chance to speak.

3. MAKING A REQUEST

☐**basic expressions:**
1. . . . *te-kudasai* (please . . .)
2. . . . *te-kudasaimasen-ka*
   . . . *te-itadakemasen-ka*
   (Would you kindly . . . ?)

☐**examples:**
1. A: *Chotto onegai-shimasu.* (Excuse me.)
   B: *Hai.*
   A: *Koko, setsumee-shite-kudasai.* (Please explain this part.)
   B: *Hai.* (All right.)
2. A: *Sumimasen, chotto ojama-shimasu.* (Excuse me, may I interrupt you?)
   B: *Hai, doozo.* (Certainly.)
   A: *Chotto wakaranai tokoro-ga arimashite . . .* (There's a part that I don't understand.)
   B: *Hai.* (Yes.)
   A: *Koko-na-n-desu-ga.* (This is the part.)
   B: *Hai.* (Yes.)
   A: *Chotto setsumee-shite-kudasaimasen-ka.* (Would you kindly explain it to me?)
   B: *Ee, ii-desu-tomo.* (Yes, certainly.)

Notes: To get someone's attention before making a request, *onegai-shimasu* is used when asking someone whose job it is to serve you. When you have to be polite, rather than saying *onegai-shimasu*, you should say *chotto ojama-shimasu* as in example 2 or *ima yoroshii-deshoo-ka* (may I interrupt you now?) or similar expressions.

When making a request, rather than asking it as a matter of course, it is regarded as polite to blame yourself for having to trouble someone; thus speaker A says in example 2 that he can't understand some part, implying his own inability.

4. ASKING FOR PERMISSION

☐basic expressions:
1. . . . *te-mo ii-deshoo-ka*
   . . . *te-mo kamaimasen-ka* (is it all right
   if . . . ?)
2. . . . *tai-n-desu-ga* . . . (I'd like to . . ., but . . .)

☐examples:
1. A: *Ashita yasunde-mo ii-deshoo-ka.* (May I be
      excused tomorrow?)
   B: *Ashita-desu-ka.* (Tomorrow?)
   A: *Ee.* (Yes.)
   B: *Maa, nantoka shimashoo.* (Well, I guess I
      will manage somehow or other.)
   A: *Doomo.* (Thank you.)
2. A: *Anoo . . .* (Excuse me.)
   B: *Nan-deshoo.* (What is it?)
   A: *Ashita chotto yooji-ga arimashite . . .* (I
      have something to do tomorrow and . . .)
   B: *Ee.* (Yes?)
   A: *Dekireba yasumasete-itadakitai-n-desu-
      ga . . .* (I'd like to be excused if possible.)
   B: *Ee, ii-desu-yo. Doozo.* (That's all right.)
   A: *Sumimasen.* (Thank you.)

Notes: *Kamaimasen-ka* and *ii-deshoo-ka* are interchangeable,
but *ii-deshoo-ka* is more polite; *yoroshii-deshoo-ka* is even
more polite.

   . . . *tai-n-desu-ga* may seem to be stating one's wishes
rather than asking for permission, but actually it is regarded
as more polite to state one's wishes and wait for the listener
to offer permission rather than to directly ask for it. The conversation in example 2 shows this type of asking for permission. In using this pattern, it is better for the speaker to
sound hesitant so that the listener will feel like stating his
opinion.

5. SHOWING DISAPPROVAL

□**basic expressions:**
1. *yoku nai-to omoimasu*; *dame-desu* (I don't think it's good; it's no good)
2. *doo-deshoo-ne*; *chotto* . . . (I wonder; a little bit . . .)

□**examples:**
1. A: *Keekaku-ga matomarimashita.* (I have made the plan.)
   B: *Soo-desu-ka. Chotto misete-kudasai.* (Is that so? Let me look at it.)
      . . . . . .
   A: *Doo-desu-ka.* (How is it?)
   B: *Koko-wa yoku nai-to omoimasu-ne.* (I don't think this part is good.)
   A: *Soo-desu-ka.* (Is that so?)
   B: *Ee, kore-ja dame-desu-yo. Hiyoo-ga kakarisu-giru.* (It won't work. It will cost too much.)
2. A: *Keekaku-ga matomarimashita.* (I have made the plan.)
   B: *Hayakatta-desu-ne. Chotto haiken shimasu.* (You've done it quickly. Please let me see it.)
      . . . . . .
   A: *Ikaga-deshoo.* (What do you think?)
   B: *Soo-desu-ne. Daitai kekkoo-desu-ga* . . . (Well, it's all right in general, but . . .)
   A: *Hai.* (Yes?)
   B: *Koko-wa chotto doo-deshoo-ne.* (I wonder about this part.)
   A: *Koko-desu-ka.* (This part?)
   B: *Ee, chotto hiyoo-no ten-de* . . . (Yes, in terms of cost, . . .)
   A: *Ah, kakarisugimasu-ka.* (Will it cost too much?)
   B: *Ee, sonna ki-ga shimasu-ga.* (Yes, I feel it will.)

Notes: The conversation in example 2 is more indirect than that in example 1, and can be recommended in social situations. When you have to be polite, it is rather difficult to show your disapproval; in such cases disapproval can be suggested by such expressions as *chotto* (*lit.* a little), *saa* (well), and *doo-deshoo-ne* (I wonder). And in pointing out a weak point, it is regarded as more agreeable to explain it with pauses as in example 2, than to say everything in one breath, as in *Koko-wa hiyoo-no ten-de mazui-to omoimasu* (I think it's not good in terms of cost).

6. REFUSAL

□**basic expressions:**
1. *dekimasen; dame-desu* (I can't; it's impossible)
2. *. . .te . . .te, sore-ni . . .* (. . .and . . ., and besides. . .)

□**examples:**
1. A: *Chotto onegai-ga aru-n-desu-ga.* (Will you do me a favor?)
   B: *Hai, nan-deshoo.* (What is it?)
   A: *Uchi-no kodomo-ni eego-o oshiete-yatte-kudasaimasen-ka.* (Won't you teach my child English?)
   B: *Ima shigoto-ga isogashii-desu-ka, warui-kedo dekimasen.* (I'm sorry but I'm busy working now, so I can't.)
2. A: *Chotto onegai-ga aru-n-desu-ga.* (Will you do me a favor?)
   B: *Hai, nan-deshoo.* (What is it?)
   A: *Uchi-no kodomo-ni eego-o oshiete-yatte-kudasaimasen-ka.* (Won't you teach my child English?)
   B: *Soo-desu-nee. . .* (Well. . .)
   A: *Onegai-shimasu.* (Please.)
   B: *Ima chotto shigoto-ga isogashii-node. . .* (I'm busy working now, so. . .)
   A: *Haa. . .* (Well. . .)
   B: *Kaisha-mo hitode-ga tarinakute. . .* (There aren't enough people working for the company and. . .)
   A: *Soo-desu-ka.* (Is that so?)
   B: *Sore-ni kono-goro tsukareyasui mon-desu-kara. . .* (And I get tired easily these days, so. . .)
   A: *Soo-desu-ka. Ja, . . .* (Is that so? Then . . .)
   B: *Doomo sumimasen.* (I'm sorry.)
   A: *Iie, murina koto-o onegai-shimashite. . .* (Oh no, I'm sorry I asked you for too much.)

Notes: Declining someone's proposal without hurting his feelings is rather difficult. As in example 2, a polite way of saying no is just giving reasons for not being able to accept rather than flatly saying no.

7. COMPLAINT

☐**basic expressions:**
1. . . .*shinaide-kudasai*; . . .*shite-wa komarimasu* (please don't. . .; you shouldn't — *lit.* I'll be troubled if. . .)
2. . . .*te*, . . .*te*, . . .*mon-desu-kara* (. . .and. . ., and because. . .)

☐**examples:**
1. A: *Ano, sumimasen-ga.* (Excuse me.)
   B: *Hai.* (Yes.)
   A: *Terebi-no oto-o amari ookiku shinaide-ku-dasai.* (Please don't have your TV on so loud.)
   B: *Hai, wakarimashita.* (All right.)
2. A: *Anoo, chotto onegai-shitai-n-desu-ga. . .* (Excuse me, would you do me a little favor?)
   B: *Hai, nan-deshoo.* (What is it?) ·
   A: *Ima shiken-de benkyoo-ga isogashikute. . .* (I have an exam coming and I'm studying hard.)
   B: *Taihen-desu-ne.* (That's tough.)
   A: *Ee, sore-de. . .* (And. . .)
   B: *Hai.* (Yes.)
   A: *Watashi-wa mawari-ga shizuka-ja nai-to ben-kyoo-dekinai mon-desu-kara. . .* (I can't study unless it's quiet around me.)
   B: *Aa, uchi-no terebi, urusai-desu-ka.* (Oh, our TV is disturbing you, isn't it?)
   A: *Ee, chotto.* (Yes, a little bit.)
   B: *Sore-wa sumimasen-deshita, ki-ga tsukana-kute.* (I'm sorry I didn't notice that.)

Notes: In polite conversations, one does not present his complaint straightforwardly. People usually prefer, as in example 2, explaining their trouble and waiting for the other to realize his fault. The important thing is not to blame the other so definitely as to corner him; it is regarded as better to bring up the matter as if it were not his fault.

8. GIVING ADVICE

□**basic expressions:**
1. . . .*ta hoo-ga ii-deshoo.* (it's better to. . .)
2. . . .*tara ikaga-desu-ka.* (it might be better to. . .)

□**examples:**
1. A: *Kaoiro-ga warui-desu-ne.* (You don't look well.)
   B: *Ee, chotto nebusoku-na-n-desu.* (Well, I haven't been sleeping well.)
   A: *Hayaku kaetta hoo-ga ii-deshoo.* (You had better go home early.)
   B: *Soo-desu-ne. Ja, soo shimashoo.* (Well, then, I'll do that.)
2. A: *Doomo okao-no iro-ga amari yoku arimasen-ne.* (You don't look very well.)
   B: *Chotto kono-goro nebusoku-deshite-ne.* (I haven't been sleeping well these days.)
   A: *Daijoobu-desu-ka.* (Are you all right?)
   B: *Ee, maa.* (I guess so.)
   A: *Soo-desu-ka. Demo, yappari kyoo-wa hayaku okaeri-ni nattara ikaga-desu-ka.* (But it might be better for you to go home early today.)
   B: *Soo-desu-nee. . .* (Well. . .)
   A: *Soo nasattara ikaga-desu-ka.* (Why don't you do that?)
   B: *Arigatoo-gozaimasu. Ja, soo sasete-itadaki-mashoo-ka.* (Thank you. Since you so kindly say so, I'll do that.)

Notes: For basic expressions 2, *doo-desu-ka* can be used in place of *ikaga-desu-ka*; this will sound less polite.

It is more polite to sound hesitant in giving advice; although advice comes from good will, it is not appropriate to offer advice before you are allowed to, to someone with whom you should be polite. Many Japanese refrain from giving advice to others, not from lack of kindness but from reserve.

9. LEAVE-TAKING

□**basic expressions:**
1. *ja, kyoo-wa kore-de shitsuree-shimasu* (then I'll leave now for today)
2. *mooshiwake nai-n-desu-ga, kore-de. . .* (I'm very sorry, but with this. . .)

□**examples:**
1. A: *Soo yuu koto-ni shimashoo-ka* (Shall we decide on it that way?)
   B: *Soo-desu-ne.* (Yes.)
   A: *Ja, kyoo-wa kore-de shitsuree-shimasu.* (Then, I'll leave now for today.)
   B: *Soo-desu-ka. Doomo arigatoo-gozaimashita.* (Is that so? Thank you very much.)
   A: *Shitsuree-shimasu.* (Good-bye.)
2. A: *Soo yuu koto-ni shimashoo-ka.* (Shall we decide on it that way?)
   B: *Soo-desu-ne.* (Yes.)
   A: *Anoo, mooshiwake nai-n-desu-ga, kore-de. . .* (Well, I'm very sorry, but with this. . .)
   B: *A, moo okaeri-desu-ka.* (Oh, are you leaving so soon?)
   A: *Ee.* (Yes.)
   B: *Mada yoroshii-ja arimasen-ka.* (Can't you stay longer?)
   A: *Ee, demo chotto yooji-ga arimashite. . .* (Thank you, but I have something to do, and. . .)
   B: *Soo-desu-ka. Ja, zannen-desu-ga.* (Is that so? That's too bad.)
   A: *Shitsuree-shimasu.* (Good-bye.)

Notes: It is rather difficult to cut short a conversation and leave, especially when conversing with a polite Japanese. Example 1 shows a case where the speakers can be business-like. In most cases you have to go through an exchange such as the one shown in example 2. Before saying *mooshiwake nai-n-desu-ga* or *sumimasen-ga* (I'm sorry), you should pause slightly and change your tone, making it sound more formal.

Such direct expressions as *moo kaerimasu* or *moo kaeru* are used only between close friends or family members, or when the speaker is angry about something.

INDEX TO WORDS, PHRASES AND SENTENCES

160